Kaplan Publishing are constantly finding new ways to make a difference to your ~~exciting online resources really d~~ different to students looking for e

D0514365

This book comes with free EN-gage online resources so that you can study anytime, anywhere.

Having purchased this book, you have access to the following online study materials:

CONTENT	ACCA (including FFA,FAB,FMA)		AAT		FIA (excluding FFA,FAB,FMA)	
	Text	Kit	Text	Kit	Text	Kit
iPaper version of the book	✓		✓	✓	✓	✓
Interactive electronic version of the book	✓					
Fixed tests / progress tests with instant answers	✓					
Mock assessments online				✓		
Material updates	✓	✓	✓	✓	✓	✓
Latest official ACCA exam questions		✓				
Extra question assistance using the signpost icon*		✓				
Timed questions with an online tutor debrief using the clock icon*		✓				
Interim assessment including questions and answers		✓			✓	
Technical articles	✓	✓			✓	✓

* Excludes F1, F2, F3, FFA, FAB, FMA

How to access your online resources

Kaplan Financial students will already have a Kaplan EN-gage account and these extra resources will be available to you online. You do not need to register again, as this process was completed when you enrolled. If you are having problems accessing online materials, please ask your course administrator.

If you are already a registered Kaplan EN-gage user go to www.EN-gage.co.uk and log in. Select the 'add a book' feature and enter the ISBN number of this book and the unique pass key at the bottom of this card. Then click 'finished' or 'add another book'. You may add as many books as you have purchased from this screen.

If you purchased through Kaplan Flexible Learning or via the Kaplan Publishing website you will automatically receive an e-mail invitation to Kaplan EN·gage online. Please register your details using this email to gain access to your content. If you do not receive the e-mail or book content, please contact Kaplan Flexible Learning.

If you are a new Kaplan EN-gage user register at www.EN-gage.co.uk and click on the link contained in the email we sent you to activate your account. Then select the 'add a book' feature, enter the ISBN number of this book and the unique pass key at the bottom of this card. Then click 'finished' or 'add another book'.

Your Code and Information

This code can only be used once for the registration of one book online. This registration and your online content will expire when the final sittings for the examinations covered by this book have taken place. Please allow one hour from the time you submit your book details for us to process your request.

Please scratch the film to access your EN-gage code.

Please be aware that this code is case-sensitive and you will need to include the dashes within the passcode, but not when entering the ISBN. For further technical support, please visit www.EN-gage.co.uk

BASIC ACCOUNTING II

Qualifications and Credit Framework

Level 2 Certificate in Accounting

British Library Cataloguing-in-Publication Data

A catalogue record for this book is available from the British Library.

Published by
Kaplan Publishing UK
Unit 2, The Business Centre
Molly Millars Lane
Wokingham
Berkshire
RG41 2QZ

ISBN: 978-0-85732-591-4

The text in this material and any others made available by any Kaplan Group company does not amount to advice on a particular matter and should not be taken as such. No reliance should be placed on the content as the basis for any investment or other decision or in connection with any advice given to third parties. Please consult your appropriate professional adviser as necessary. Kaplan Publishing Limited and all other Kaplan group companies expressly disclaim all liability to any person in respect of any losses or other claims, whether direct, indirect, incidental, consequential or otherwise arising in relation to the use of such materials.

Printed and bound in Great Britain.

We are grateful to the Association of Accounting Technicians for permission to reproduce past assessment materials and example tasks based on the new syllabus. The solutions to past answers and similar activities in the style of the new syllabus have been prepared by Kaplan Publishing.

CONTENTS

STUDY TEXT AND WORKBOOK

KAPLAN PUBLISHING

INTRODUCTION

HOW TO USE THESE MATERIALS

These Kaplan Publishing learning materials have been carefully designed to make your learning experience as easy as possible and to give you the best chance of success in your AAT assessments.

They contain a number of features to help you in the study process.

The sections on the Unit Guide, the Assessment and Study Skills should be read before you commence your studies.

They are designed to familiarise you with the nature and content of the assessment and to give you tips on how best to approach your studies.

STUDY TEXT

This study text has been specially prepared for the revised AAT qualification introduced in July 2010.

It is written in a practical and interactive style:

- key terms and concepts are clearly defined

- all topics are illustrated with practical examples with clearly worked solutions based on sample tasks provided by the AAT in the new examining style

- frequent activities throughout the chapters ensure that what you have learnt is regularly reinforced

- practice workbook activities can be completed at the end of each chapter

WORKBOOK

The workbook comprises:

Practice activities at the end of each chapter with solutions at the end of the text, to reinforce the work covered in each chapter.

The questions are divided into their relevant chapters and students may either attempt these questions as they work through the textbook, or leave some or all of these until they have completed the textbook as a final revision of what they have studied.

ICONS

The study chapters include the following icons throughout.

They are designed to assist you in your studies by identifying key definitions and the points at which you can test yourself on the knowledge gained.

Definition

These sections explain important areas of Knowledge which must be understood and reproduced in an assessment

Example

The illustrative examples can be used to help develop an understanding of topics before attempting the activity exercises

Activity

These are exercises which give the opportunity to assess your understanding of all the assessment areas.

KAPLAN PUBLISHING

UNIT GUIDE

Basic accounting II is the second of the two financial accounting assessments at level 2.

Maintaining petty cash records (skills)

1 credit

Maintaining and reconciling the cash book (skills)

2 credits

Maintaining the journal (skills)

2 credits

Maintaining control accounts (skills)

1 credit

Banking procedures (skills)

1 credit

The following unit is assessed in both Basic accounting I and Basic accounting II, and will only be awarded once both assessments have been achieved

Principles of recording and processing financial transactions (knowledge)

2 credits

Purpose of the units

The AAT has stated that this unit is designed to build on Basic Accounting I which focuses on the double entry bookkeeping system up to an initial trial balance. Basic Accounting II looks in more detail at the cash book and petty cash book and introduces the reconciliation of control accounts. The learner will also be required to make adjustments through the journal and re-draft the initial trial balance once adjustments have been made.

Learning objectives

On completion of these units the learner will be able to:

- Complete a petty cash voucher
- Maintain an analysed petty cash book
- Maintain the petty cash balance
- Maintain a three column analysed cash book
- Reconcile a bank statement with the cash book
- Understand the use of the journal
- Open a new set of double entry bookkeeping records using the journal
- Use the journal to correct errors disclosed and not disclosed by the trial balance
- Create and clear a suspense account using the journal
- Use the journal to record other transactions
- Understand control accounts
- Prepare sales and purchase ledger and tax control accounts
- Reconcile sales and purchase ledger and tax control accounts

Learning Outcomes and Assessment criteria

The unit consists of fifteen learning outcomes, three for Knowledge and twelve for Skills, which are further broken down into Assessment criteria. These are set out in the following table with Learning Outcomes in bold type and Assessment criteria listed underneath each Learning Outcome. Reference is also made to the relevant chapter within the text.

Knowledge

To perform this unit effectively you will need to have successfully achieved Basic Accounting I, and know and understand the following:

Chapter

1   Understand the role of the books of prime entry

1.1   Outline the purpose, content and format of the books   1
      of prime entry

1.2   Outline the purpose and content of a range of   1
      business documents to include:

- petty cash voucher

- invoice

- credit note

- remittance advice

1.3   Identify when authorisation is required   1

1.4   Explain how transactions are entered in the following   1
      books of prime entry

- sales and sales returns day books

- purchases and purchases returns day books

- cash book

- petty cash book

2   Understand the principles of coding

2.1   Describe the need for a coding system for financial   1
      transactions within a double entry bookkeeping system

2.2   Describe the use of coding within a filing system   1

Skills

To perform this unit effectively you will need to be able to do the following.

Chapter

Maintaining control accounts

1 Prepare sales and purchase ledger and tax control accounts

1.1	Prepare a sales ledger control account from information extracted from the books of prime entry	3
1.2	Balance the sales ledger control account	3
1.3	Prepare a purchase ledger control account from information extracted from the books of prime entry	3
1.4	Balance the purchase ledger control account	3
1.5	Prepare a tax control account from information extracted from the books of prime entry	2

2 Reconcile sales and purchase ledger and tax control accounts

2.1	Reconcile the balance on the sales ledger control account with a list of debtors	3
2.2	Reconcile the balance on the purchase ledger control account with a list of creditors	3
2.3	Reconcile the balances on the tax control account	2

Maintaining the journal

1 Open a new set of double entry book keeping records using the journal

1.1	Prepare the journal entries to open a double entry set of bookkeeping records for a new and existing business	3
1.2	Record the journal entries in the ledger accounts	3

2 Use the journal to correct errors disclosed and not disclosed by the trial balance

2.1	Identify and record journal entries in the general ledger to correct errors not disclosed by the trial balance	4

KAPLAN PUBLISHING

THE ASSESSMENT

The format of the assessment

The assessment will be divided into two sections, with 6 tasks in section 1 and 8 in section 2.

Learners will normally be assessed by computer based assessment (CBA), and will be required to demonstrate competence in both sections of the assessment.

Time allowed

The time allowed for this assessment is **two hours.**

Terminology

The AAT fully adopted IFRS terminology on 1st January 2012. The IFRS terms do not impact greatly on the Basic Accounting II paper. The listing provided gives the IFRS term (AAT preferred term) and the related UK GAAP term. You should ensure you are familiar with the following terms:

UK GAAP	IFRS
Trade debtors / Debtors	Trade receivables / Receivables
Trade creditors / Creditors	Trade payables / Payables
Debtors ledger control account Sales ledger control account	Receivables ledger control account Sales ledger control account
Creditors ledger control account Purchases ledger control account	Payables ledger control account Purchases ledger control account
Sales / Purchases ledger	Sales / Purchases ledger
Sales tax / VAT	Sales tax / VAT
Fixed asset	Non-current asset
Stock	Inventory
Bad debt	Irrecoverable debt

Also note, under payroll the terms "PAYE" and "National Insurance Contributions (NIC)" may also be known as "Income Tax" and "Social Security" respectively.

STUDY SKILLS

Preparing to study

Devise a study plan

Determine which times of the week you will study.

Split these times into sessions of at least one hour for study of new material. Any shorter periods could be used for revision or practice.

Put the times you plan to study onto a study plan for the weeks from now until the assessment and set yourself targets for each period of study – in your sessions make sure you cover the whole course, activities and the associated questions in the workbook at the back of the manual.

If you are studying more than one unit at a time, try to vary your subjects as this can help to keep you interested and see subjects as part of wider knowledge.

When working through your course, compare your progress with your plan and, if necessary, re-plan your work (perhaps including extra sessions) or, if you are ahead, do some extra revision / practice questions.

Effective studying

Active reading

You are not expected to learn the text by rote, rather, you must understand what you are reading and be able to use it to pass the assessment and develop good practice.

A good technique is to use SQ3Rs – Survey, Question, Read, Recall, Review:

1   **Survey the chapter**

    Look at the headings and read the introduction, knowledge, skills and content, so as to get an overview of what the chapter deals with.

2   **Question**

    Whilst undertaking the survey ask yourself the questions you hope the chapter will answer for you.

3   Read

Read through the chapter thoroughly working through the activities.

4   Recall

At the end of each section and at the end of the chapter, try to recall the main ideas of the section / chapter without referring to the text. This is best done after short break of a couple of minutes after the reading stage.

5   Review

Check that your recall notes are correct.

You may also find it helpful to re-read the chapter to try and see the topic(s) it deals with as a whole.

Note taking

Taking notes is a useful way of learning, but do not simply copy out the text.

The notes must:

- be in your own words
- be concise
- cover the key points
- be well organised
- be modified as you study further chapters in this text or in related ones.

Trying to summarise a chapter without referring to the text can be a useful way of determining which areas you know and which you don't.

Three ways of taking notes

1   Summarise the key points of a chapter

2   Make linear notes

A list of headings, subdivided with sub-headings listing the key points.

If you use linear notes, you can use different colours to highlight key points and keep topic areas together.

Use plenty of space to make your notes easy to use.

3   Try a diagrammatic form

The most common of which is a mind map.

To make a mind map, put the main heading in the centre of the paper and put a circle around it.

Draw lines radiating from this to the main sub-headings which again have circles around them.

Continue the process from the sub-headings to sub-sub-headings.

Highlighting and underlining

You may find it useful to underline or highlight key points in your study text – but do be selective.

You may also wish to make notes in the margins.

Revision phase

Kaplan has produced material specifically designed for your final examination preparation for this unit.

These include pocket revision notes and a bank of revision questions specifically in the style of the new syllabus.

Further guidance on how to approach the final stage of your studies is given in these materials.

Further reading

In addition to this text, you should also read the "Student section" of the "Accounting Technician" magazine every month to keep abreast of any guidance from the examiners.

Accounting for sales – summary

1

Introduction

We have previously studied the double entry bookkeeping for sales and receipts in detail within Basic Accounting I (BAI). It is essential that you have completed and achieved BAI before you commence your studies for Basic Accounting II (BAII).

When studying BAI we concentrated on the basic entries so that the double entry would be clear. It is now time to build on these basic entries and study these transactions again using more realistic material.

KNOWLEDGE

- Recap from BAI

2.1 Explain why it is important for an organisation to have a formal document retention policy

2.2 Identify the different types of documents that may be stored

CONTENTS

1 The sales day book
2 The analysed sales day book
3 The sales returns day book
4 Posting to the sales ledger
5 The analysed cash book
6 The three column cash book
7 Document retention policies

1   The sales day book

The sales day book is a book of prime entry where credit sales are recorded. This example provides us with a recap of the material from our BAI studies.

💡 Example

Given below are three invoices that have been sent out by your organisation today. You are required to record them in the sales day book

	INVOICE
	A.J. Broom & Company Limited
Invoice to:	59 Parkway
T J Builder	Manchester
142/148 Broadway	M2 6EG
Oldham	Tel: 0161 560 3392
OD7 6LZ	Fax: 0161 560 5322

Deliver to:	Invoice no: 69489
As above	Tax point: 23 August 20X3
	Sales tax reg no: 625 9911 58
	Delivery note no: 68612
	Account no: SL21

Code	Description	Quantity	Sales tax rate	Unit price	Amount excl of sales tax
			%	£	£
874 KL7	Brown Brick Roof Tiles	40	20	43.95	1,758.00
					1,758.00
Trade discount 5%					87.90
					1,670.10
Sales tax					323.99
Total amount payable					1,994.09
Deduct discount of 3% if paid within 14 days					

		INVOICE			
Invoice to: McCarthy & Sons Shepherds Moat Manchester M6 9LF **Deliver to:** As above		**A.J. Broom & Company Limited** 59 Parkway Manchester M2 6EG Tel: 0161 560 3392 Fax: 0161 560 5322 Invoice no: 69490 Tax point: 28 August 20X3 Sales tax reg no: 625 9911 58 Delivery note no: 68610 Account no: SL08			

Code	Description	Quantity	Sales tax rate	Unit price	Amount excl of sales tax
			%	£	£
617 BB8	Red Wall Bricks	400	20	2.10	840.00
294 KT6	Insulation Brick	3	20	149.90	449.70
					1,289.70
Trade discount 4%					51.58
					1,238.12
Sales tax					247.62
Total amount payable					1,485.74

	INVOICE
Invoice to: Trevor Partner Anderson House Bank Street Manchester M1 9FP	**A.J. Broom & Company Limited** 59 Parkway Manchester M2 6EG Tel: 0161 560 3392 Fax: 0161 560 5322
Deliver to: As above	Invoice no: 69491 Tax point: 28 August 20X3 Sales tax reg no: 625 9911 58 Delivery note no: 68613 Account no: SL10

Code	Description	Quantity	Sales tax rate	Unit price	Amount excl of sales tax
			%	£	£
611 TB4	Bathroom Tiles	160	20	5.65	904.00
					904.00
Trade discount 2%					18.08
					885.92
Sales tax					173.64
Total amount payable					1,059.58
Deduct discount of 2% if paid within 21 days					

Solution

SALES DAY BOOK

Date	Invoice No	Customer name	Code	Total £	Sales tax £	Net £
28/08/X3	69489	T J Builder	SL21	1,994.09	323.99	1,670.10
28/08/X3	69490	McCarthy & Sons	SL08	1,485.74	247.62	1,238.12
28/08/X3	69491	Trevor Partner	SL10	1,059.58	173.64	885.92

KAPLAN PUBLISHING

2 The analysed sales day book

2.1 Introduction

Many organisations analyse their sales into different groups. This may be analysis by different products or by the geographical area in which the sale is made. If the sales are eventually to be analysed in this manner in the accounting records then they must be analysed in the original book of prime entry, the sales day book.

 **Example**

You work for an organisation that makes sales to five different geographical regions. You are in charge of writing up the sales day book and you have listed out the details of the invoices sent out yesterday, 15 August 20X1. They are given below and must be entered into the sales day book and the totals of each column calculated. The sales tax rate in use is 20%.

The invoice details are as follows:

	£
Invoice number 167 – France	
Worldwide News – (Code W5)	
Net total	2,500.00
Sales tax	500.00
Gross	3,000.00
Invoice number 168 – Spain	
Local News – (Code L1)	
Net total	200.00
Sales tax	40.00
Gross	240.00
Invoice number 169 – Germany	
The Press Today – (Code P2)	
Net total	300.00
Sales tax	60.00
Gross	360.00

Invoice number 170 – Spain	
Home Call – (Code H1)	
Net total	200.00
Sales tax	40.00
Gross	240.00
Invoice number 171 – France	
Tomorrow – (Code T1)	
Net total	100.00
Sales tax	20.00
Gross	120.00
Invoice number 172 – Russia	
Worldwide News – (Code W5)	
Net total	3,000.00
Sales tax	600.00
Gross	3,600.00

Solution

SALES DAY BOOK

Date	Invoice no	Customer name	Code	Total	Sales tax	Russia	Poland	Spain	Germany	France
				£	£	£	£	£	£	£
15/08/X1	167	Worldwide	W5	3,000.00	500.00					2,500.00
	168	Local News	L1	240.00	40.00			200.00		
	169	The Press Today	P2	360.00	60.00				300.00	
	170	Home Call	H1	240.00	40.00			200.00		
	171	Tomorrow	T1	120.00	20.00					100.00
	172	Worldwide News	W5	3,600.00	600.00	3,000.00				
				7,560.00	1,260.00	3,000.00	–	400.00	300.00	2,600.00

When you have totalled the columns you can check your additions by 'cross-casting'. If you add together the totals of all of the analysis columns and the sales tax column, they should total the figure in the 'Total' column.

Activity 1

Sweepings Ltd is a wall covering manufacturer. It produces four qualities of wallpaper:

01 – Anaglypta

02 – Supaglypta

03 – Lincrusta

04 – Blown Vinyl

Francis is a sales ledger clerk and he is required to write up the sales day book each week from the batch of sales invoices he receives from the sales department.

He has just received this batch of sales invoices which show the following details. All sales are standard-rated for sales tax.

Invoice no	Date	Customer	Description	Amount (incl sales tax) £
1700	06.09.X1	Gates Stores	Anaglypta, 188 rolls	480.00
1701	06.09.X1	Texas	Blown Vinyl, 235 rolls	1,800.00
1702	07.09.X1	Dickens	Blown Vinyl, 188 rolls	1,440.00
1703	07.09.X1	Hintons DIY	Supaglypta, 470 rolls	1,920.00
1704	08.09.X1	Co-op Stores	Anaglypta, 94 rolls	240.00
1705	08.09.X1	B & Q Stores	Lincrusta, 125 rolls	1,200.00
1706	09.09.X1	Ferris Decor	Supaglypta, 235 rolls	960.00
1707	09.09.X1	Ferris Decor	Blown Vinyl, 94 rolls	720.00
1708	10.09.X1	Homestyle	Lincrusta, 25 rolls	240.00
1709	10.09.X1	Quick Style	Anaglypta, 47 rolls	120.00

Show how this information would appear in the sales day book given below, including the totals of the relevant columns.

SALES DAY BOOK									
Date	Invoice	Customer	Code	Total	Sales tax	Group 01	Group 02	Group 03	Group 04
				£	£	£	£	£	£

Activity 2

Given below are the totals from the analysed sales day book for an organisation for a week.

Sales day book	Gross	Sales tax	Sales Type 1	Sales Type 2
	£	£	£	£
Totals	8,652.00	1,442.00	4,320.00	2,890.00

You are required to post these totals to the general ledger accounts given below: SLCA account

SLCA account

£		£

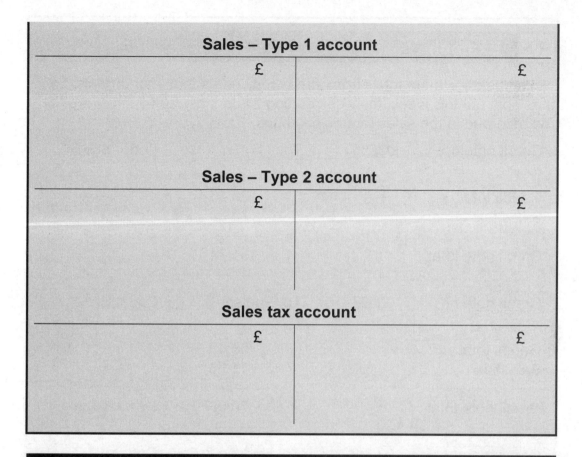

Sales – Type 1 account

£	£

Sales – Type 2 account

£	£

Sales tax account

£	£

3 The sales returns day book

3.1 Introduction

When goods are returned by customers and credit notes sent out then these credit notes are also recorded in their own book of prime entry, the sales returns day book.

3.2 Sales returns day book

The sales returns day book is effectively the reverse of the sales day book but will have the same entries, the total of the credit note, including sales tax, the sales tax element and the net amount, excluding the sales tax.

💡 Example

Given below are the totals from three credit notes that your organisation has sent out this week, the week ending 21 January 20X4. They are to be recorded in the sales returns day book.

Credit note no:	03556	To: J Slater & Co	Code: SL67

	£
Goods total	126.45
Sales tax	25.29
Credit note total	151.74

Credit note no:	03557	To: Paulsons	Code: SL14

	£
Goods total	58.40
Sales tax	11.68
Credit note total	70.08

Credit note no:	03558	To: Hudson & Co	Code: SL27

	£
Goods total	104.57
Sales tax	20.91
Credit note total	125.48

Solution

Sales returns day book						
Date	Credit note no	Customer name	Code	Total	Sales tax	Net
				£	£	£
21/01/X4	03556	J Slater & Co	SL67	151.74	25.29	126.45
21/01/X4	03557	Paulsons	SL14	70.08	11.68	58.40
21/01/X4	03558	Hudson & Co	SL27	125.48	20.91	104.57

3.3 Analysed sales returns day book

If the business keeps an analysed sales day book then it will also analyse its sales returns day book in exactly the same manner.

> **Example**
>
> In an earlier example we considered the sales day book for an organisation that makes sales to five different geographical regions. The sales returns day book would also be analysed into these geographical regions. The details of two credit notes issued this week are given and are to be written up in the sales returns day book. Today's date is 21 October 20X6.
>
> Credit note no: 0246 – Poland   To: Russell & Sons   Code: R3
>
> | | £ |
> |---|---|
> | Goods total | 85.60 |
> | Sales tax | 17.12 |
> | | 102.72 |
>
> Credit note no: 0247 – Germany   To: Cleansafe   Code: C7
>
> | | £ |
> |---|---|
> | Goods total | 126.35 |
> | Sales tax | 25.27 |
> | | 151.62 |
>
> **Solution**
>
> **Sales returns day book**
>
> | Date | Credit | Customer | Code | Total | Sales tax | Russia | Poland | Spain | Germany | France |
> |---|---|---|---|---|---|---|---|---|---|---|
> | 21/10/X6 | 0246 | Russell & Sons | R03 | 102.72 | 17.12 | | 85.60 | | | |
> | 21/10/X6 | 0247 | Cleansafe | C07 | 151.62 | 25.27 | | | | 126.35 | |
> | | | | | | | | | | | |

Activity 3

A business analyses its sales into Product 1 sales and Product 2 sales. During the week ending 14 March 20X4 the following credit notes were sent out to customers.

CN3066   £120.00 plus sales tax – Product 2, Customer K Lilt, Code L04

CN3067   £16.00 plus sales tax – Product 1, Customer J Davis, Code D07

CN3068   £38.00 plus sales tax – Product 1, Customer I Oliver, Code O11

CN3069   £80.00 plus sales tax – Product 2, Customer D Sharp, Code S02

Enter the credit notes in the analysed sales returns day book given below and total the day book for the week.

Sales returns day book

Date	Credit note no	Customer name	Code	Total	Sales tax	Product 1	Product 2
				£	£	£	£

Activity 4

Given below are the totals from the analysed sales returns day book for an organisation for a week:

Date	Customer name	Credit note no	Code	Total £	Sales tax £	Sales Type 1 £	Sales Type 2 £
25/09/X2				601.80	100.30	327.00	174.50

Post these totals to the general ledger accounts.

4 Posting to the sales ledger

As well as posting the totals from the books of prime entry to the general ledger accounts each individual invoice and credit note must also be posted to the individual customer's account in the sales ledger. You must remember that the sales ledger is sometimes referred to as the subsidiary (sales) ledger.

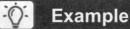 Example

Here is an account from the sales ledger of Frosty Limited, a glass manufacturer which specialises in glassware for the catering trade.

Account name:		Account code:	
	£		£

You have taken over writing up the sales ledger because the ledger clerk has been ill for several months.

You have gathered together the following information about sales. The customer is a new customer whose name is Arthur Pickering. The account code will be SP05.

Sales invoices

Date	Invoice number	Gross	Sales tax	Net
		£	£	£
02/05/X1	325	598.06	99.67	498.39
03/06/X1	468	243.98	40.66	203.32
15/06/X1	503	115.84	19.30	96.54
16/06/X1	510	49.74	8.29	41.45
24/06/X1	CN048	28.32	4.72	23.60
17/07/X1	604	450.51	75.08	375.43

Solution

Account name: Arthur Pickering			Account code: SP05		
		£			£
02/05/X1	Inv 325	598.06	25/06/X1	CN048	28.32
03/06/X1	Inv 468	243.98			
15/06/X1	Inv 503	115.84			
16/06/X1	Inv 510	49.74			
17/07/X1	Inv 604	450.51			

Remember that sales invoices are always entered on the debit side of the customer's account and credit notes on the credit side of the account.

5 The analysed cash book

5.1 Introduction

In order to revise the layout of the cash receipts book consider the following example.

Cash receipts book for the week commencing 15 September 20X4

Date	Narrative	Total	Sales tax	SLCA	Cash/ cheque sales	Discount allowed
		£	£	£	£	£
15 Sept	Paying-in slip 584	653.90		653.90		
16 Sept	Paying-in slip 585	864.60		864.60		
17 Sept	Paying-in slip 586	954.98	11.24	887.54	56.20	
18 Sept	Paying-in slip 587	559.57		559.57		
19 Sept	Paying-in slip 588	238.18	31.69	48.00	158.49	
		3,271.23	42.93	3,013.61	214.69	

The bankings are a mixture of cash sales and cheques from receivables. The sales tax is just the sales tax on the cash/cheque sales. There are no discounts.

Check that the three analysis column totals add back to the total column total.

Example

Returning to the cash receipts book, post the totals to the general ledger accounts.

Cash receipts book

Date	Narrative	Total	Sales tax	Receiv-ables	Cash/ cheque sales	Discount allowed
		£	£	£	£	£
15 Sept	Paying-in slip 584	653.90		653.90		
16 Sept	Paying-in slip 585	864.60		864.60		
17 Sept	Paying-in slip 586	954.98	11.24	887.54	56.20	
18 Sept	Paying-in slip 587	559.57		559.57		
19 Sept	Paying-in slip 588	238.18	31.69	48.00	158.49	
		3,271.23	42.93	3,013.61	214.69	

Solution

The double entry for posting the cash receipts book totals is:

		£	£
DR	Bank account	3,271.23	
CR	Sales tax account		42.93
	Sales ledger control account		3,013.61
	Sales account		214.69

Bank account

	£		£
Cash receipts book (CRB)	3,271.23		

Sales tax account

	£		£
		CRB	42.93

Sales ledger control account

	£		£
		CRB	3,013.61

Sales account		
£		£
	CRB	214.69

Note that the description of each transaction is the primary record that it came from, the cash receipts book, shortened to CRB.

Activity 5

The cheques received from customers of Passiflora Products Ltd, a small company which produces herbal remedies and cosmetics and supplies them to shops and beauty parlours, for a week are given below:

Cheques received:

	Paying-in slip/customer	Amount	Discount allowed
		£	£
01/5/X6	Paying-in slip 609		
	Natural Beauty	11,797.05	176.95
	Grapeseed	417.30	6.26
	New Age Remedies	6,379.65	95.69
	The Aromatherapy Shop	9,130.65	136.96
03/5/X6	Paying-in slip 610		
	Comfrey Group	5,689.20	85.34
	Natural Elegance	2,056.89	30.85
08/5/X6	Paying-in slip 611		
	The Herbalist	8,663.45	129.95
12/5/X6	Paying-in slip 612		
	Edwards Pharmacy	106.42	
	Healthworks	17,213.94	258.21
19/5/X6	Paying-in slip 613		
	The Beauty Box	11,195.85	167.94
	Crystals	54.19	
25/5/X6	Paying-in slip 614		
	The Village Chemist	7,662.55	114.94
29/5/X6	Paying-in slip 615		
	Brewer Brothers	2,504.61	37.57
30/5/X6	Paying-in slip 616		
	Lapis Lazuli	112.58	
31/5/X6	Paying-in slip 617		
	Lorelei	5,618.40	84.27
	Spain & Co, Chemists	197.93	

KAPLAN PUBLISHING

Required:

(a) Enter the totals for each paying-in slip (including discounts) into the cash receipts book given below.

(b) Total the cash receipts book and post the totals for the month to the general ledger accounts given.

(a) **Cash receipts book**

Date	Narrative	Total	Sales tax	Receivables	Other	Discount
		£	£	£	£	£

(b) **General ledger**

Sales ledger control account

£		£

Discount allowed account

£		£

Activity 6

Given below are the details of paying-in slip 609 from the previous activity, Passiflora Products Ltd. You are required to enter the details in the sales ledger accounts given.

Paying-in slip 609

	Amount	Discount allowed
	£	£
Natural Beauty	11,797.05	176.95
Grapeseed	417.30	6.26
New Age Remedies	6,379.65	95.69
The Aromatherapy Shop	9,130.65	136.96

Natural Beauty

	£		£
Opening balance	17,335.24		

The Aromatherapy Shop

	£		£
Opening balance	12,663.42		

New Age Remedies

	£		£
Opening balance	6,475.34		

Grapeseed

	£		£
Opening balance	423.56		

6 The three column cash book

6.1 Introduction

Within Basic Accounting I (BAI), the analysed cash receipts book and cash payments book were looked at separately.

A "three column" cash book is the terminology used when the cash book details cash, bank and discount transactions, as seen in BAI.

It is important to remember that discounts allowed and discounts received appear within the cash book for memorandum purposes only and therefore still need to be entered appropriately into the double entry system.

Activity 7

Cash book – Debit side

Date	Details	Discount £	Bank £
30 Nov	Balance b/f		10,472
30 Nov	SMK Ltd	300	12,000

(a) What will be the TWO entries in the sales ledger?

Sales Ledger

Account name	Amount £	Debit / Credit

(b) What will be the THREE entries in the general ledger?

General ledger

Account name	Amount £	Debit / Credit

7 Document retention policies

7.1 Introduction

Throughout the studies for Basic Accounting I and II we will have seen many documents that businesses produce. It is a legal requirement that all financial documents, and some non-financial documents, must be kept by a business for six years. Therefore it is essential that a business has a secure and organised method of filing such information, to ensure that they can be located easily.

7.2 Reasons for document retention

Documents must be kept for three main reasons:

- in order that they could be inspected by the tax authorities (HM Revenue and Customs) in a tax inspection;

- in order that they could be inspected by the tax authorities (HM Revenue and Customs) in a sales tax (VAT) inspection;

- in order that they could be used as evidence in any legal action.

8 Summary

In this chapter we have pulled together into one place all the main documents and double entry for the sales cycle. If you have had any trouble with any of these points, you should refer again to the relevant chapters of the textbook for Basic Accounting I where the double entry is explained in basic terms. Basic Accounting II is building on our knowledge from Basic Accounting I.

Answers to chapter activities

Activity 1

SALES DAY BOOK

Date	Invoice	Customer	Code	Total	Sales tax	Group 01	Group 02	Group 03	Group 04
				£	£	£	£	£	£
06/09/X1	1700	Gates Stores		480.00	80.00	400.00			
06/09/X1	1701	Texas		1,800.00	300.00				1,500.00
07/09/X1	1702	Dickens		1,440.00	240.00				1,200.00
07/09/X1	1703	Hintons DIY		1,920.00	320.00		1,600.00		
08/09/X1	1704	Co-op Stores		240.00	40.00	200.00			
08/09/X1	1705	B & Q Stores		1,200.00	200.00			1,000.00	
09/09/X1	1706	Ferris Decor		960.00	160.00		800.00		
09/09/X1	1707	Ferris Decor		720.00	120.00				600.00
10/09/X1	1708	Homestyle		240.00	40.00			200.00	
10/09/X1	1709	Quick Style		120.00	20.00	100.00			
				9,120.00	1,520.00	700.00	2,400.00	1,200.00	3,300.00

Activity 2

SLCA

	£		£
SDB	8,652.00		

Sales – Type 1 account

	£		£
		SDB	4,320.00

Sales – Type 2 account

	£		£
		SDB	2,890.00

Sales tax account

	£		£
		SDB	1,442.00

Activity 3

SALES RETURNS DAY BOOK

Date	Credit note no	Customer name	Code	Total £	Sales tax £	Product 1 £	Product 2 £
14/3	3066	K Lilt	L04	144.00	24.00		120.00
14/3	3067	J Davis	D07	19.20	3.20	16.00	
14/3	3068	I Oliver	O11	45.60	7.60	38.00	
14/3	3069	D Sharp	S02	96.00	16.00		80.00
				304.80	50.80	54.00	200.00

Activity 4

Sales ledger control account

	£			£
		SRDB		601.80

Sales returns – Type 1

	£		£
SRDB	327.00		

Sales returns – Type 2

	£		£
SRDB	174.50		

Sales tax account

	£		£
SRDB	100.30		

Activity 5

(a) Cash receipts book

Date	Narrative	Total £	Sales tax £	SLCA £	Others £	Discount £
01/05/X6	Cheques – 609	27,724.65		27,724.65		415.86
03/05/X6	Cheques – 610	7,746.09		7,746.09		116.19
08/05/X6	Cheques – 611	8,663.45		8,663.45		129.95
12/05/X6	Cheques – 612	17,320.36		17,320.36		258.21
19/05/X6	Cheques – 613	11,250.04		11,250.04		167.94
25/05/X6	Cheques – 614	7,662.55		7,662.55		114.94
29/05/X6	Cheques – 615	2,504.61		2,504.61		37.57
30/05/X6	Cheques – 616	112.58		112.58		
31/05/X6	Cheques – 617	5,816.33		5,816.33		84.27
		88,800.66	–	88,800.66	–	1,324.93

(b) General ledger

Sales ledger control account

	£		£
		CRB	88,800.66
		CRB – discount allowed	1,324.93

Discount allowed account

	£		£
CRB	1,324.93		

Activity 6

Natural Beauty

	£		£
Opening balance	17,335.24	CRB	11,797.05
		CRB – discount	176.95

The Aromatherapy Shop

	£		£
Opening balance	12,663.42	CRB	9,130.65
		CRB – discount	136.96

New Age Remedies			
	£		£
Opening balance	6,475.34	CRB	6,379.65
		CRB – discount	95.69
Grapeseed			
	£		£
Opening balance	423.56	CRB	417.30
		CRB – discount	6.26

Activity 7

Cashbook – Debit side

Date	Details	Discount £	Bank £
30 Nov	Balance b/f		10,472
30 Nov	SMK Ltd	300	12,000

(a)   What will be the TWO entries in the sales ledger?

Sales Ledger

Account name	Amount £	Debit / Credit
SMK Ltd	12,000	Credit
SMK Ltd	300	Credit

(b)   What will be the THREE entries in the general ledger?

General Ledger

Account name	Amount £	Debit / Credit
SLCA	12,000	Credit
Discount allowed	300	Debit
SLCA	300	Credit

9 Test your knowledge

Workbook Activity 8

Your organisation receives a number of cheques from receivables through the post each day and these are listed on the cheque listing. It also makes some cash sales each day which include sales tax at the standard rate.

Today's date is 28 April 20X1 and the cash sales today were £240.00 including sales tax. The cheque listing for the day is given below:

Cheque listing 28 April 20X1

G Heilbron	£108.45
L Tessa	£110.57 – settlement discount of £3.31 taken
J Dent	£210.98 – settlement discount of £6.32 taken
F Trainer	£ 97.60
A Winter	£105.60 – settlement discount of £3.16 taken

An extract from the customer file shows the following:

Customer	Sales ledger code
J Dent	SL17
G Heilbron	SL04
L Tessa	SL15
F Trainer	SL21
A Winter	SL09

Required:

(a) Write up the cash receipts book given below; total each of the columns of the cash receipts book and check that they cross-cast

(b) Post the totals of the cash receipts book to the general ledger accounts.

(c) Post the individual receipts to the sales ledger.

Cash receipts book							
Narrative	SL Code	Discount £	Cash £	Bank £	Sales tax £	Cash Sales £	SLCA £

Workbook Activity 9

There are 5 receipts to be entered into Longley Ltd's cash receipts book.

Cash receipts

From Irlam Transport – £468.00 (inc sales tax)

From Paulson Haulage – £216.00 (inc sales tax)

From Mault Motors – £348.00 (inc sales tax)

Cheques received from credit customers

From James John Ltd – £579.08 (discount of £24.39 taken)

From Exilm & Co – £456.74 (discount of £19.80 taken)

Required:

Write up the cash receipts book given below; total each of the columns of the cash receipts book and check that they cross cast.

Cash receipts book						
Narrative	Discount £	Cash £	Bank £	Sales tax £	Cash Sales £	SLCA £

Workbook Activity 10

Indicate whether each of the following statements is true or false.

	True/False
Documents can be disposed of as soon as the year end accounts are prepared	
Documents cannot be inspected by anyone outside the business	
Documents can be used as legal evidence in any legal actions	
Businesses must keep an aged receivable analysis as part of their financial documents	
Businesses do not need to keep copies of invoices	
Businesses need to keep copies of their bank statements available for inspection	

Accounting for purchases – summary 2

Introduction

As well as recapping accounting for sales as seen in chapter 1, we also need to recap on the techniques learned in Basic Accounting I for purchases.

KNOWLEDGE
• Recap from BAI

CONTENTS

1 The purchases day book
2 Returns of goods
3 Accounting entries in the general ledger
4 Accounting entries in the purchases ledger
5 The impact of sales tax
6 Settlement discounts
7 The three column cashbook

1 The purchases day book

1.1 Introduction

In the purchases day book, the purchase invoices are normally given an internal invoice number and are also recorded under the supplier's purchase ledger code and possibly the type of purchase.

1.2 Authorisation stamp

This is often done by stamping an authorisation stamp or grid stamp onto the invoice once it has been thoroughly checked and the relevant details entered onto the authorisation stamp. A typical example of an authorisation stamp is shown below:

Purchase order no	04618
Invoice no	04821
Cheque no	
Account code	PL06
Checked	L Finn
Date	23/02/X2
ML account	07

1.3 Entries on the authorisation stamp

At this stage of entering the invoice in the purchases day book it has been checked to the purchase order and the delivery note, therefore the purchase order number is entered onto the authorisation stamp.

The purchase invoice will then be allocated an internal invoice number which will be sequential and therefore the next number after the last invoice entered into the purchases day book.

At this stage the invoice will not necessarily have been authorised for payment, therefore the cheque number will not yet be entered onto the authorisation stamp.

The purchase invoice details such as trade and settlement discounts should have been checked to the supplier's file to ensure that the correct percentages have been used and at this point the supplier's purchases ledger code can be entered onto the authorisation stamp.

The person checking the invoice should then sign and date the authorisation stamp to show that all details have been checked.

Finally, the general ledger account code should be entered. We have seen that in some businesses a simple three column purchases day book will be used with a total, sales tax and net column. In such cases all of the invoices will be classified as 'purchases' and will have the general ledger code for the purchases account.

However, if an analysed purchases day book is used then each analysis column will be for a different type of expense and will have a different general ledger code.

If your organisation does have an authorisation stamp procedure then it is extremely important that the authorisation is correctly filled out when the invoice has been checked. Not only is this evidence that the invoice is correct and is for goods or services that have been received, it also provides vital information for the accurate accounting for this invoice.

Example

Given below are three purchase invoices received and the authorisation stamp for each one. They are to be entered into the purchases day book. Today's date is 25 April 20X1.

INVOICE

Invoice to:
Keller Bros
Field House
Winstead
M16 4PT

Deliver to:
Above address

Anderson Wholesale
Westlife Park
Gripton
M7 1ZK
Tel: 0161 439 2020
Fax: 0161 439 2121

Invoice no:	06447
Tax point:	20 April 20X1
Sales tax reg no:	432 1679 28
Account no:	SL14

Code	Description	Quantity	Sales tax rate	Unit price	Amount excl of sales tax
			%	£	£
PT417	Grade A Compost	7 tonnes	20	15.80	110.60
					110.60
Trade discount 5%					5.53
					105.07
Sales tax					21.01
Total amount payable					126.08

Purchase order no	34611
Invoice no	37240
Cheque no	
Account code	PL14
Checked	C Long
Date	25/04/X1
GL account	020

INVOICE

Invoice to:
Keller Bros
Field House
Winstead
M16 4PT

Deliver to:
Above address

Better Gardens Ltd

Broom Nursery
West Lane
Farforth M23 4LL
Tel: 0161 380 4444
Fax: 0161 380 6128

Invoice no:	46114
Tax point:	21 April 20X1
Sales tax reg no:	611 4947 26
Account no:	K03

Code	Description	Quantity	Sales tax rate	Unit price	Amount excl of sales tax
			%	£	£
B4188	Tulip bulbs	28 dozen	20	1.38	38.64
B3682	Daffodil bulbs	50 dozen	20	1.26	63.00
					101.64
Sales tax					19.71
Total amount payable					121.35
Deduct discount of 3% if paid within 14 days					

Purchase order no	34608
Invoice no	37241
Cheque no	
Account code	PL06
Checked	C Long
Date	25/04/X1
GL account	020

INVOICE

Invoice to: Keller Bros Field House Winstead M16 4PT	**Winterton Partners** **28/32 Coleman Road** **Forest Dene** **M17 3AT** Tel: 0161 224 6760 Fax: 0161 224 6761
Deliver to: Above address	Invoice no: 121167 Tax point: 22 April 20X1 Sales tax reg no: 980 3012 74 Account no: SL44

Code	Description	Quantity	Sales tax rate	Unit price	Amount excl of sales tax
			%	£	£
A47BT	Seedlings	120	20	0.76	91.20
					91.20
Trade discount 7%					6.38
					84.82
Sales tax					16.62
Total amount payable					101.44
Deduct discount of 2% if paid within 14 days					

Purchase order no	34615
Invoice no	37242
Cheque no	
Account code	PL23
Checked	C Long
Date	25/04/X1
GL account	020

Solution

Purchases day book						
Date	Invoice no	Code	Supplier	Total	Sales tax	Net
				£	£	£
25/04/X1	37240	PL14	Anderson Wholesale	126.08	21.01	105.07
25/04/X1	37241	PL06	Better Gardens Ltd	121.35	19.71	101.64
25/04/X1	37242	PL23	Winterton Partners	101.44	16.62	84.82

Note that the net total is the invoice amount after deducting any trade discount as the trade discount is a definite reduction in the list price of the goods. At this stage any settlement discount is ignored as it will not necessarily have been decided whether or not to take advantage of the settlement discount.

Activity 1

You are a purchases clerk for Robins, a soft drink manufacturer. Here is part of the layout of the purchases day book.

Purchases day book									
Date	Invoice no	Code	Supplier	Total	Sales tax	01	02	03	04
				£	£	£	£	£	£

01 represents purchases of parts or raw materials for manufacture

02 represents advertising expenditure

03 represents entertaining expenditure

04 represents purchases of non-current assets

Here are five documents that are to be written up in the purchases day book on 10.11.X2 as necessary.

Document 1

No: 511 X

	SALES INVOICE		*Drip Farm*

To: Robins Ltd
        Softdrink House
        Wembley
        London
        NW16 7SJ

**Lover's Lane
Norwich NO56 2EZ**

**Tax point: 7.11.X2
Sales tax Reg No: 566
0122 10**

Quantity	Description	Sales tax rate	Price/unit	Total
50 litre drum	Apple juice (inferior)	20%	£2/litre	100.00
			Sales tax	20.00
				120.00

Grid stamp on reverse of invoice

Invoice no	4221
Account code	DF2
Checked	R Robins
Date	9.11.X2
GL account	01

Document 2

| Sales Invoice | Inv No: 5177 |

DAILY NEWS PLC

Europe Way
Southampton
SO3 3BZ

Tax point 5.11.X2
Sales tax Reg No: 177 0255 01

To: Robins Ltd
     Softdrink House
     Wembley
     London
     NW16 7SJ

Sale details:

			£
4 line advertisement			
3 weeks	04.10.X2 @ £100/week		
	11/10.X2	Net price	300.00
	18.10.X2	Sales tax	60.00
			360.00

Grid stamp on reverse of invoice.

Invoice no	4222
Account code	DN1
Checked	R Robins
Date	9.11.X2
GL account	02

Document 3

RECEIPT

Yellow River Restaurant

9/11/12

Received with thanks the sum of
£17.50

T W Wang

Document 4

SALES ORDER 562		
		Robins Ltd Softdrink House Wembley LONDON NW16 7SJ
BTEB Stores Gateshead		
Quantity	**Description**	**Price**
20 cases	0.75 bottles of Norfolk apple juice	£2/bottle

Document 5

SALES INVOICE P261

STANDARD MACHINES

Starlight Boulevard, Milton Keynes

MK51 7LY

To: Robins Ltd
      Softdrink House
      Wembley
      LONDON
      NW16 7SJ

Tax point: 6.11.X2

Sales tax Reg No: 127 0356 02

Quantity	Description	Sales tax	Price (£)/unit
1	Bottling machine	20%	2,000
		Sales tax	400
			2,400

Grid stamp on reverse of invoice.

Invoice no.	4223
Account code	SM4
Checked	R Robins
Date	9.11.X2
GL account	04

2 Returns of goods

2.1 Introduction

Returns may be made for various reasons, e.g.

- faulty goods;
- excess goods delivered by supplier;
- unauthorised goods delivered.

All returned goods must be recorded on a returns outwards note.

2.2 Credit notes

The return should not be recorded until the business receives a credit note from the supplier. This confirms that there is no longer a liability for these goods. A credit note from a supplier is sometimes requested by the organisation issuing a debit note.

The credit note should be checked for accuracy against the returns outwards note. The calculations and extensions on the credit note should also be checked in just the same way as with an invoice.

2.3 Purchases returns day book

When credit notes are received from suppliers they are normally recorded in their own primary record, the purchases returns day book. This has a similar layout to a purchases day book. If the purchases day book is analysed into the different types of purchase that the organisation makes then the purchases returns day book will also be analysed in the same manner.

Example

Today, 5 February 20X5, three credit notes have been passed as being checked. The details of each credit note and the authorisation stamp are given below. The credit note details are to be entered into the purchases returns day book.

From Calderwood & Co	£
Goods total	16.80
Sales tax	3.36
Credit note total	20.16

Purchase order no	41120
Credit note	C461
Cheque no	–
Account code	053
Checked	J Garry
Date	05/02/X5
GL account	02

From Mellor & Cross	£
Goods total	104.50
Less: Trade discount 10%	10.45
	94.05
Sales tax	18.81
Credit note total	112.86

Purchase order no	41096
Credit note	C462
Cheque no	–
Account code	259
Checked	J Garry
Date	05/02/X5
ML account	02

From Thompson Bros Ltd	£
Goods total	37.60
Less: Trade discount 5%	1.88
	35.72
Sales tax	7.14
Credit note total	42.86

Purchase order no	41103
Credit note	C463
Cheque no	–
Account code	360
Checked	J Garry
Date	05/02/X5
GL account	01

Solution

Purchases returns day book									
Date	Credit note no	Code	Supplier	Total £	Sales tax £	01 £	02 £	03 £	04 £
05/02/X5	C461	053	Calderwood & Co	20.16	3.36		16.80		
05/02/X5	C462	259	Mellor & Cross	112.86	18.81		94.05		
05/02/X5	C463	360	Thompson Bros Ltd	42.86	7.14	35.72			

Note that it is the credit note total which is entered into the total column and the sales tax amount into the sales tax column. The amount entered into the analysis columns is the goods total less the trade discount. The analysis column is taken from the general ledger code on the authorisation stamp.

Activity 2

A newsagents shop has received the following invoices. Write them up in the purchases day book using the format provided. The last internal invoice number to be allocated to purchase invoices was 114.

1.1.X1	Northern Electric – invoice	£120 including sales tax
	Northern Gas – invoice	£230 (no sales tax)
2.1.X1	Post Office Ltd – invoice	£117.00 (no sales tax)
	Northern Country – invoice	£48 including sales tax
3.1.X1	South Gazette – invoice	£360 including sales tax

The supplier codes are as follows:

Northern Country (a newspaper)	N1
Northern Electric	N2
Northern Gas	N3
Post Office Ltd	P1
South Gazette (a newspaper)	S1

Purchases day book

Date	Invoice no	Code	Supplier	Total	Sales tax	Goods for resale	Heat and light	Postage and stationery
				£	£	£	£	£

3 Accounting entries in the general ledger

3.1 Introduction

The accounting entries that are to be made in the general ledger are the same as those that have been considered in Basic Accounting I and are made from the totals of the columns in the purchases day book and purchases returns day book.

3.2 Analysed purchases day book

If an analysed purchases day book is being used then there will be a debit entry in an individual purchases or expense account for each of the analysis column totals.

Remember that these totals are the net of sales tax purchases/expenses totals.

Example

Reproduced below is a purchases day book for the first week of February 20X5. Each column has been totalled and it must be checked that the totals of the analysis columns agree to the 'Total' column. Therefore you should check the following sum:

	£
01	744.37
02	661.23
03	250.45
04	153.72
Sales tax	296.14
	2,105.91

Purchases day book

Date	Invoice no	Code	Supplier	Total £	Sales tax £	01 £	02 £	03 £	04 £
20X5									
1 Feb	3569	265	Norweb	151.44	25.24	126.20			
2 Feb	3570	053	Calderwood & Co	98.60			98.60		
3 Feb	3571	259	Mellor & Cross	675.15	112.52		562.63		
4 Feb	3572	360	Thompson Bros Ltd	265.71	44.28	221.43			
5 Feb	3573	023	Cooplin Associates	18.90				18.90	
	3574	056	Heywood Suppliers	277.86	46.31			231.55	
	3575	395	William Leggett	46.33	7.72				38.61
	3576	271	Melville Products	374.29	62.38	311.91			
	3577	301	Quick-Bake	101.79	16.96	84.83			
	3578	311	Roger & Roebuck	138.13	23.02				115.11
				2,148.20	338.43	744.37	661.23	250.45	153.72

The totals of the purchases day book will now be posted to the general ledger accounts.

Solution

Purchase ledger control account

	£		£
		PDB	2,105.91

Sales tax account

	£		£
PDB	296.14		

Purchases – 01 account

	£		£
PDB	744.37		

Purchases – 02 account

	£		£
PDB	661.23		

Purchases – 03 account

	£		£
PDB	250.45		

Purchases – 04 account

	£		£
PDB	153.72		

3.3 Purchases returns day book

The purchases returns day book is kept in order to record credit notes received by the business. The totals of this must also be posted to the general ledger.

Example

Given below is a purchases returns day book for the week. The totals are to be posted to the general ledger accounts. Sales tax is at 20%.

Purchases day book									
Date	Credit note no	Code	Supplier	Total	Sales tax	01	02	03	04
				£	£	£	£	£	£
20X3									
4 May	CN 152	PL21	Julian R Partners	132.00	22.00		110.00		
6 May	CN 153	PL07	S T Trader	81.60	13.60			68.00	
8 May	CN 154	PL10	Ed Associates	70.32	11.72		58.60		
8 May	CN 155	PL03	Warren & Co	107.52	17.92	89.60			
				391.44	65.24	89.60	168.60	68.00	–

Solution

First, check that each of the column totals add back to the total column total:

	£
Sales tax	65.24
01	89.60
02	168.60
03	68.00
04	–
	391.44

Then post the totals to the general ledger accounts:

Purchases ledger control account

	£		£
Purchases return day book (PRDB)	391.44		

Sales tax account

	£		£
		PRDB	65.24

Purchases returns – 01

	£		£
		PRDB	89.60

Purchases returns – 02

	£		£
		PRDB	168.60

Purchases returns – 03

	£		£
		PRDB	68.00

If the purchases returns day book is analysed then there will be an account in the general ledger for each different category of purchases returns.

KAPLAN PUBLISHING

Activity 3

Given below is the purchases day book. You are required to check the total of each analysis column and that the total of each analysis column agrees to the total column, and then to enter the totals in the correct general ledger accounts.

Purchases day book

Date	Invoice no	Code	Supplier	Total £	Sales tax £	Goods for sale £	Heat and light £	Postage and stationery £
01.01.X1	115	N2	Northern Electric	120.00	20.00		100.00	
	116	N3	Northern Gas	230.00			230.00	
02.01.X1	117	P1	Post Office	117.00				117.00
	118	N1	Northern Country	48.00	8.00	40.00		
03.01.X1	119	S1	South Gazette	360.00	60.00	300.00		
				875.00	88.00	340.00	330.00	117.00

4 Accounting entries in the purchases ledger

4.1 Purchases ledger

As well as posting the totals from the books of prime entry to the general ledger accounts, each individual invoice and credit note must also be posted to the individual supplier's account in the purchases ledger (also referred to as the subsidiary (purchases) ledger.

Example

Here is an account from the purchases ledger of Frosty Limited.

Account name: **Code:**

Date	Transaction	£	Date	Transaction	£

We will write up the account for Jones Brothers, account number PJ06. This is a new supplier.

Frosty Limited has only been trading for a short time and is not yet registered for sales tax.

Purchase invoices and credit notes

02.5.X1	9268	£638.26
06.6.X1	9369	£594.27
15.6.X1	9402	£368.24
17.6.X1	C Note 413	£58.62
19.6.X1	9568	£268.54

Solution

Account name: Jones Brothers   **Account number:** PJ06

Date	Transaction	£	Date	Transaction	£
17.6.X1	Credit note 413	58.62	02.5.X1	Invoice 9268	638.26
			06.6.X1	Invoice 9369	594.27
			15.6.X1	Invoice 9402	368.24
			19.6.X1	Invoice 9568	268.54

Each purchase invoice from the Purchases Day Book must be entered on the credit side of that individual suppliers account in the purchases ledger. Any credit notes recorded in the Purchases Returns Day Book must be recorded on the debit side of the supplier's account. Where there is sales tax involved the amount to be recorded for an invoice or credit note is the gross amount or sales tax inclusive amount.

5 The impact of sales tax

5.1 Introduction

Having looked at the accounting for purchase invoices and credit notes, we will now move on to consider the accounting for payments to suppliers. First we will consider the impact of sales tax in this area.

When writing up the payments side of the cash book sales tax must be considered.

Any payments to suppliers or payables included in the Purchases ledger column need have no analysis for sales tax as the sales tax on the purchase was recorded in the purchases day book when the invoice was initially received.

However any other payments on which there is sales tax must show the gross amount in the Total column, the sales tax in the sales tax column and the net amount in the relevant expense column.

KAPLAN PUBLISHING

Example

Peter Craddock is the cashier for a business which manufactures paper from recycled paper. The payments that were made for one week in September are as follows:

15 September	Cheque no 1151 to K Humphrey (credit supplier)	£1,034.67
	Cheque no 1152 to Y Ellis (credit supplier)	£736.45
	Cheque no 1153 to R Phipps (credit supplier)	£354.45
	Standing order for rent	£168.15
	Direct debit to the electricity company	£130.98
	(including sales tax of £22.92)	
16 September	Cheque no 1154 to L Silton (credit supplier)	£1,092.75
	Cheque no 1155 to the insurance company	£103.18
17 September	Cheque no 1156 to F Grange (credit supplier)	£742.60
	Cheque no 1157 to Hettler Ltd for cash purchases	£420.00 plus sales tax
18 September	Cheque no 1158 to J Kettle (credit supplier)	£131.89
19 September	BACS payment of wages	£4,150.09
	Cheque no 1159 to Krane Associates for cash purchases	£186.00 plus sales tax

Enter these transactions into the cash payments book, total the columns and post the totals to the general ledger.

Solution

Date	Details	Cheque no	Total £	Sales tax £	PLCA £	Cash purchases £	Rent £	Electricity £	Wages £	Insurance £
15/9	K Humphrey	1151	1,034.67		1,034.67					
	Y Ellis	1152	736.45		736.45					
	R Phipps	1153	354.45		354.45					
	Rent	SO	168.15				168.15			
	Electricity	DD	130.98	22.92				108.06		
16/9	L Silton	1154	1,092.75		1,092.75					
	Insurance	1155	103.18							103.18
17/9	F Grange	1156	742.60		742.60					
	Hettler Ltd	1157	504.00	84.00		420.00				
18/9	J Kettle	1158	131.89		131.89					
	Wages	BACS	4,150.09						4,150.09	
19/9	Krane Ass	1159	223.20	37.20		186.00				
			9,372.41	144.12	4,092.81	606.00	168.15	108.06	4,150.09	103.18

The analysis column totals should add back to the Total column – this must always be done to check the accuracy of your totalling.

	£
Sales tax	144.12
Purchases ledger	4,092.81
Cash purchases	606.00
Rent	168.15
Electricity	108.06
Wages	4,150.09
Insurance	103.18
	9,372.41

Purchase ledger control account

		£		£
19/9	CPB	4,092.81		

Sales tax account

		£		£
19/9	CPB	144.12		

Purchases account

		£		£
19/9	CPB	606.00		

Electricity account

		£		£
19/9	CPB	108.06		

Salaries account

		£		£
19/9	CPB	4,150.09		

Rent account

		£		£
19/9	CPB	168.15		

Insurance account

		£		£
19/9	CPB	103.18		

All of the entries in the general ledger accounts are debit entries. The credit entry is the total column of the cash payments book and these individual debit entries form the double entry.

6 Settlement discounts

6.1 Introduction

If a business takes advantage of settlement discounts on items purchased, the discount is treated as income as it is a benefit to the business i.e. although the invoice is paid earlier, the amount paid is less than the invoice net amount due to the discount.

Settlement (cash) discounts are recorded in a memorandum column in the cash book. The memorandum column does not form part of the double entry. It requires an entire piece of double entry itself (see below).

The business must record these settlement discounts. Trade discounts are not recorded in the cash book.

An extra column is included in the analysed cash payments book. This should be the final right hand column.

Example

The following four payments have been made today, 12 June 20X6:

Cheque number 22711 B Caro	Purchases ledger code CL13
	£342.80 after taking a settlement discount of £14.20
Cheque number 22712 S Wills	Cash purchases of £240.00 inclusive of sales tax
Cheque number 22713 P P & Co	Purchases ledger code CL22 £116.40
Cheque number 22714 W Potts	Purchases ledger code CL18 £162.84

The relevant purchases ledger accounts are shown below

B Caro (CL 13)

	£		£
		PDB Invoice	357.00

W Potts (CL 18)

	£		£
PRDB Credit note	10.00	PDB Invoice	172.84

P P & Co (CL 22)

	£		£
		PDB Invoice	116.40
		PDB Invoice	121.27

In this example we will:

- write up the cash payments book for the day;

- total the columns to check that they add back to the total of the Total column;

- enter the totals in the general ledger;

- write up each individual entry in the purchases ledger.

Solution

Date	Details	Cheque	Code	Total £	Sales tax £	PLCA £	Cash purchases £	Other £	Discounts £
12 Jun	B Caro	22711	CL13	342.80		342.80			14.20
	S Wills	22712		240.00	40.00		200.00		
	PP&Co	22713	CL22	116.40		116.40			
	W Potts	22714	CL18	162.84		162.84			
				862.04	40.00	622.04	200.00	–	14.20

Total Check

	£
Purchases ledger	622.04
Cash purchases	200.00
Sales tax	40.00
	862.04

Note that the discount received column is not included in the total check as this is simply a memorandum column.

General ledger

Purchase ledger control account

	£		£
CPB	622.04		
CPB – discount	14.20		

Purchases account

	£		£
CPB	200.00		

Sales tax account

	£		£
CPB	40.00		

Discounts received account

	£		£
		CPB	14.20

When posting the cash payments book to the general ledger there are two distinct processes. Firstly enter the totals of each of the analysis columns as debits in their relevant accounts in the general ledger. Then do the double entry for the discounts received – debit the purchase ledger control account and credit the discounts received account.

Purchases ledger

B Caro (CL 13)

		£			£
CPB	Payment	342.80	PDB	Invoice	357.00
CPB	Discount	14.20			

Note that the discount is entered here as well as the cash payment

W Potts (CL 18)

		£			£
PRDB	Credit note	10.00	PDB	Invoice	172.84
CPB	Payment	162.84			

P P & Co (CL 22)

		£			£
CPB	Payment	116.40	PDB	Invoice	116.40
			PDB	Invoice	121.27

📝 Activity 4

Given below is a completed cash payments book. You are required to:

(a) Total each of the columns and check that the totals add across to the total column.

(b) Post the totals to the general ledger accounts given.

(c) Post the individual payable entries to the payables' accounts in the purchases ledger, also given.

Date	Details	Cheque no	Code	Total £	Sales tax £	PLCA £	Cash purchases £	Wages £
1/7	G Hobbs	34	PL14	325.46		325.46		
1/7	Purchases	35	ML03	65.40	11.40		57.00	
2/7	Purchases	36	ML03	50.59	8.43		42.16	
3/7	P Taylor	37	PL21	157.83		157.83		
3/7	S Dent	38	PL06	163.58		163.58		
4/7	K Smith	39	ML07	24.56				24.56
				———	———	———	———	———
				———	———	———	———	———

7 The three column cashbook

7.1 Introduction

As we have revised receipts side the three column cashbook in the previous chapter, the following activity will revise this approach with the payments side.

Activity 5

Cashbook – Credit side

Date	Details	Sales tax £	Bank £
30 Nov	Motor expenses	40	240
30 Nov	Wages		6,200
30 Nov	HMRC		4,750

What will be the FOUR entries in the general ledger?

General ledger

Account name	Amount £	Debit / Credit

8 Summary

In this chapter we have pulled together into one place all the main documents and double entry for the purchases cycle. If you have had any trouble with any of these points, you should refer again to the Basic Accounting I Study Text where the double entry is explained.

Answers to chapter activities

Activity 1

Purchases day book

Date	Invoice no	Code	Supplier	Total £	Sales tax £	01 £	02 £	03 £	04 £
10/11/X2	4221	DF2	Drip Farm	120.00	20.00	100.00			
10/11/X2	4222	DN1	Daily News plc	360.00	60.00		300.00		
10/11/X2	4223	SM4	Standard Machines	2,400.00	400.00				2,000.00
				2,880.00	480.00	100.00	300.00	–	2,000.00

Document 3 receipt is not a purchase invoice, it is a receipt for cash paid.

Document 4 is a sales order to supply 20 cases of bottled juice. It is not a purchase invoice so would not appear in the purchases day book.

Activity 2

Purchases day book

Date	Invoice no	Code	Supplier	Total £	Sales tax £	Goods for resale £	Heat and light £	Postage and stationery £
01.01.X1	115	N2	Northern Electric	120.00	20.00		100.00	
	116	N3	Northern Gas	230.00	–		230.00	
02/01.X1	117	P1	Post Office Ltd	117.00	–			117.00
	118	N1	Northern Country	48.00	8.00	40.00		
03/01/X1	119	S1	South Gazette	360.00	60.00	300.00		
				875.00	88.00	340.00	330.00	117.00

Activity 3

	£
Goods for resale	340.00
Heat and light	330.00
Postage and stationery	117.00
Sales tax	88.00
	———
Total	875.00
	———

Purchases (goods for resale)

	£		£
PDB	340.00		

Heat and light

	£		£
PDB	330.00		

Postage and stationery

	£		£
PDB	117.00		

Sales tax

	£		£
PDB	88.00		

Purchases ledger control account

	£		£
		PDB	875.00

Activity 4

(a) Cash payments book

Date	Details	Cheque no	Code	Total £	Sales tax £	PLCA £	Cash purchases £	Wages £
1/7	G Hobbs	34	PL14	325.46		325.46		
1/7	Purchases	35	ML03	68.40	11.40		57.00	
2/7	Purchases	36	ML03	50.59	8.43		42.16	
3/7	P Taylor	37	PL21	157.83		157.83		
3/7	S Dent	38	PL06	163.58		163.58		
4/7	K Smith	39	ML07	24.56				24.56
				790.42	19.83	646.87	99.16	24.56

Check that totals add across:

	£
Sales tax	19.83
Purchases ledger	646.87
Cash purchases	99.16
Wages	24.56
	790.42

(b) General ledger accounts

Purchases ledger control account

	£		£
CPB	646.87		

Cash purchases account

	£		£
CPB	99.16		

Wages account

	£		£
CPB	24.56		

Sales tax account

	£		£
CPB	19.83		

(c) Purchases ledger

G Hobbs			PL14
	£		£
CPB	325.46		

P Taylor			PL21
	£		£
CPB	157.83		

S Dent			PL06
	£		£
CPB	163.58		

Activity 5

Cashbook – Credit side

Date	Details	Sales tax £	Bank £
30 Nov	Motor expenses	40	240
30 Nov	Wages		6,200
30 Nov	Tax authorities		4,750

What will be the FOUR entries in the general ledger?

General Ledger

Account name	Amount £	Debit / Credit
Motor expenses	200	Debit
Sales tax control account	40	Debit
Wages	6,200	Debit
Sales tax control account	4,750	Debit

9 Test your knowledge

✏️ Workbook Activity 6

Given below is the cheque listing for a business for the week ending 12 March

Cheque payment listing

Supplier	Code	Cheque number	Cheque amount £	Discount taken £
Homer Ltd	PL12	03648	168.70	5.06
Forker & Co	PL07	03649	179.45	5.38
Cash purchases		03650	342.00	
Print Associates	PL08	03651	190.45	
ABG Ltd	PL02	03652	220.67	6.62
Cash purchases		03653	200.40	
G Greg	PL19	03654	67.89	

The cash purchases include sales tax at standard rate 20%.

You are required to:

- enter the payments into the cash payments book and total each of the columns;

- post the totals to the general ledger accounts given;

- post the individual entries to the purchases ledger accounts given.

CASH PAYMENTS BOOK

Date	Details	Code	Discount £	Cash £	Bank £	Sales tax £	PLCA £	Cash purchases £	Other £

General ledger

Purchases ledger control account

	£				£
		5/3	Balance b/d		4,136.24

Sales tax account

	£				£
		5/3	Balance b/d		1,372.56

Purchases account

		£			£
5/3	Balance b/d	20,465.88			

Discounts received account

	£				£
		5/3	Balance b/d		784.56

Purchases ledger

ABG Ltd   PL02

	£				£
		5.3	Balance b/d		486.90

Forker & Co   PL07

	£				£
		5/3	Balance b/d		503.78

Print Associates   PL08

	£				£
		5/3	Balance b/d		229.56

Homer Ltd   PL12

	£				£
		5/3	Balance b/d		734.90

G Greg   PL19

	£				£
		5/3	Balance b/d		67.89

Workbook Activity 7

There are 7 payments to be entered into JR Ltd's cash payments book.

Cash payments

To JD & Co – £96.00 (inc sales tax)

To LJ Ltd – £240.00 (inc sales tax)

To MK Plc – £60.00 (inc sales tax)

Cheque payments

To credit supplier TB Ltd – £68.89 (discount of £2.52 taken)

To credit supplier CF Ltd – £156.72 (discount of £3.16 taken)

Electricity – £90.00 (ignore sales tax)

Stationery – £84.00 (inc sales tax)

Required:

Write up the cash payments book given below; total each of the columns of the cash payments book and check that they cross cast.

Cash payments book							
Narrative	Discount £	Cash £	Bank £	Sales tax £	Cash Purchases £	PLCA £	Expenses £

Workbook Activity 8

You have been given the following extracts from Jacobsen & Co's books of prime entry for the past quarter. Sales tax is at 20%.

Sales day-book
Net:	£400,000
Sales tax:	£80,000
Gross:	£480,000

Purchases day-book
Net:	£210,000
Sales tax:	£42,000
Gross:	£252,000

Sales returns day-book
Net:	£30,000
Sales tax:	£6,000
Gross:	£36,000

Purchases returns day-book
Net:	£9,600
Sales tax:	£1,920
Gross:	£11,520

Cash receipts book
Net cash sales:	£840
Sales tax:	£168
Gross cash sales:	£1,008

Cash payments book
Net cash purchases:	£1,200
Sales tax:	£240
Gross cash purchases:	£1,440

Required:

What will be the entries in the sales tax control account to record the sales tax transactions in the quarter? Show clearly the closing balance b/d on the account stating whether or not it is a balance owing to the tax authorities or owing from the tax authorities.

Sales tax control

	£		£

Ledger balances and control accounts

3

Introduction

In this chapter we will be finding the correct ledger account balances by revising balancing off ledger accounts (covered in Basic Accounting I) as the basis for drafting an initial trial balance. In particular, we will be looking at ways of ensuring the accuracy of the balances for receivables (sales ledger control account) and payables (purchases ledger control account).

KNOWLEDGE	CONTENTS
5.1 Describe the reasons for maintaining the journal	1 Balancing ledger accounts
5.2 Describe the content and format of the journal	2 Opening balances
5.3 Give examples of the types of transactions that might be entered into the bookkeeping system by using the journal:	3 Accounting for receivables
	4 Sales ledger control account reconciliation
– irrecoverable debt	5 Accounting for payables
6.1 Describe the purpose of control accounts as a checking device to aid management and help identify bookkeeping errors	6 Purchases ledger control account reconciliation
	7 Cause of the difference
6.2 Describe the specific purpose of the following control accounts	8 Batch control
– sales ledger	9 The sales tax control account
– purchases ledger	
6.3 Explain why it is important to reconcile the sales and purchases ledger control accounts regularly	

SKILLS

1.1 Prepare a sales ledger control account from information extracted from the books of prime entry

1.2 Balance the sales ledger control account

1.3 Prepare a purchases ledger control account from information extracted from the books of prime entry

1.4 Balance the purchases ledger control account

1.5 Prepare a tax control account from information extracted from the books of prime entry

2.1 Reconcile the balance on the sales ledger control account with a list of receivables

2.2 Reconcile the balance on the purchases ledger control account with a list of payables

2.3 Reconcile the balances on the tax control account

4.1 Prepare journal entries to write off an irrecoverable debt

4.2 Enter the journal entries in the general ledger to write off an irrecoverable debt including the sales tax (e.g. VAT) where appropriate

KAPLAN PUBLISHING

1 Balancing ledger accounts

1.1 Introduction

The purpose of maintaining double entry ledger accounts is to provide information about the transactions and financial position of a business. Each type of transaction is gathered together and recorded in the appropriate ledger account, for example all sales are recorded in the sales account. Then at intervals it will be necessary to find the total of each of these types of transactions.

This is done by balancing each ledger account. This has been covered earlier in your studies but is worth revising here, by attempting Activity 1.

Activity 1

You are required to balance off the following ledger accounts:

Sales ledger control account

	£		£
SDB – invoices	5,426.23	CRB	3,226.56
		Discounts allowed	315.57

Sales tax account

	£		£
PDB	846.72	SDB	1,036.54

Sales account

	£		£
		SDB	2,667.45
		SDB	1,853.92

Opening balances

2.1 Introduction

If an account has a balance on it at the end of a period then it will have the same balance at the start of the next period. This is known as an opening balance.

2.2 Debit or credit?

The key to determining whether an opening balance on a ledger account is a debit or a credit is to understand the general rules for debit and credit balances. This can be expressed in the assessment either as a journal, or by entering the amount directly onto the ledger account.

2.3 Debit and credit balance rules

The mnemonic DEAD/CLIC will help you determine if an entry should be made on the debit side or on the credit side of a ledger account

Ledger account	
Debit:	**Credit:**
• Expenses	• Liabilities
• Assets	• Income
• Drawings	• Capital

💡 Example

You are told that the opening balance on the sales ledger control account is £33,600, the opening balance on the purchases account is £115,200 and the opening balance on the purchases ledger control account is £12,700.

You are required to enter these into the relevant ledger accounts.

Solution

Sales ledger control account			
	£		£
Balance brought forward	33,600		

	Purchases account		
	£		£
Balance brought forward	115,200		

	Purchases ledger control account		
	£		£
		Balance brought forward	12,700

Assets and expenses normally have opening debit balances. Liabilities and income normally have opening credit balances.

2.4 Journals

A journal entry is a written instruction to the bookkeeping to enter a double entry into the general ledger accounts. It is shown below in its most basic form, although the journal voucher itself is explained later in this chapter.

Example

Record the journal entries needed in the general ledger to account for the following balances.

Sales ledger control account	33,600
Purchases	115,200
Purchases ledger control account	12,700
Sales	138,240
Rent and Rates	2,140

Solution

Sales ledger control account	33,600	Debit
Purchases	115,200	Debit
Purchases ledger control account	12,700	Credit
Sales	138,240	Credit
Rent and Rates	2,140	Debit

The total of the debit entries should equal the total of the credit entries.

Activity 2

Would the balances on the following accounts be debit or credit balances?

(a)   Sales account

(b)   Discounts allowed account

(c)   Discounts received account

(d)   Wages expense account

Activity 3

The following are the opening balances for a new business. Complete the journal to record these balances.

Account name	Amount £	Debit / Credit
Bank overdraft	6,975	
Cash	275	
Sales tax payable	2,390	
Motor vehicles	10,500	
Plant and machinery	25,700	
Loan from bank	12,000	
Motor expenses	1,540	
Rent and rates	2,645	
Miscellaneous expenses	725	

Activity 4

The following transactions all occurred on 1 December 20X1 and have been entered into the relevant books of prime entry (given below). However, no entries have yet been made into the ledger system. Sales tax has been calculated at a rate of 20%.

Purchases day book

Date	Details	Invoice no	Total	Sales tax	Purchases	Stationery
			£	£	£	£	
20X1						
1 Dec	Bailey Limited	T151	240	40	200	
1 Dec	Byng & Company	10965	960	160	800	
1 Dec	Office Supplies Ltd	34565	336	56		280
1 Dec	O'Connell Frames	FL013	5,040	840	4,200	
	Totals		6,576	1,096	5,200	280

Purchases returns day book

Date	Details	Invoice no	Total	Sales tax	Purchases	Stationery
			£	£	£	£	
20X1						
1 Dec	O'Connell Frames	CO11	2,160	360	1,800	
1 Dec	Office Supplies Ltd	CR192	48	8		40
	Totals		2,208	368	1,800	40

Sales day book

Date	Details	Invoice no	Total	Sales tax	Sales
			£	£	£
20X1					
1 Dec	Bentley Brothers	H621	1,680	280	1,400
1 Dec	J & H Limited	H622	4,320	720	3,600
1 Dec	Furniture Galore	H623	4,800	800	4,000
1 Dec	The Sofa Shop	H624	2,640	440	2,200
	Totals		13,440	2,240	11,200

Opening balances

The following are some of the balances in the accounting records and are all relevant to you at the start of the day on 1 December 20X1:

	£
Credit Suppliers	
Bailey Limited	11,750
Byng & Company	1,269
Office Supplies Limited	4,230
O'Connell Frames	423
PLCA	82,006
SLCA	180,312
Purchases	90,563
Sales	301,492
Purchases returns	306
Stationery	642
Discounts received	50
Sales tax (credit balance)	17,800

Receipts on 1 December 20X1

	Total £
Lili Chang (cash sale including sales tax)	600
Bentley Brothers (credit customer)	5,875

Cheque issued

	Total £
Bailey Limited (in full settlement of debt of £819)	799

Task 1

Enter the opening balances listed above into the following accounts, blanks of which are provided on the following pages:

Task 2

Using the data shown above, enter all the relevant transactions into the accounts in the purchases ledger and general ledger. Entries to the sales ledger for receivables are not required.

Task 3

Enter the receipts and payments shown above into the cash book given on the following pages.

Task 4

Transfer any relevant sums from the cash book into the purchases ledger for payables and general ledger.

Task 5

Balance off all of the accounts and the cash book, showing clearly the balances carried down. The opening cash balance was £3,006. Find the closing balance on the cash book.

Tasks 1, 2, 4 and 5

Purchases ledger

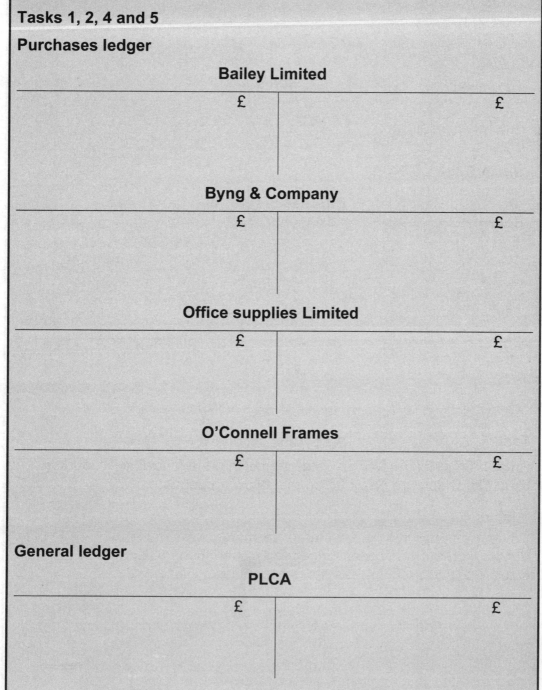

Bailey Limited

	£		£

Byng & Company

	£		£

Office supplies Limited

	£		£

O'Connell Frames

	£		£

General ledger

PLCA

	£		£

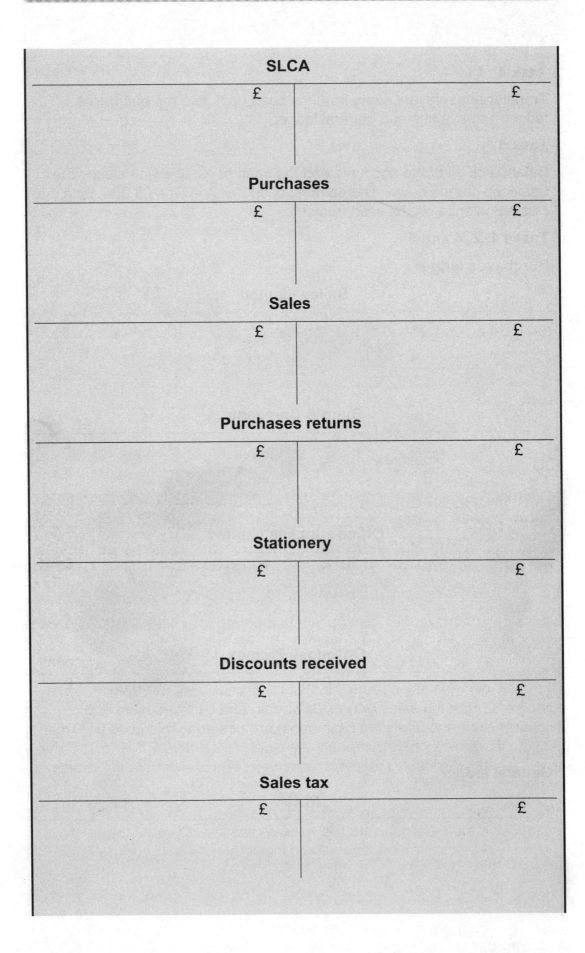

SLCA

£		£

Purchases

£		£

Sales

£		£

Purchases returns

£		£

Stationery

£		£

Discounts received

£		£

Sales tax

£		£

Tasks 3, 4 and 5

Cash receipts book

Date	Narrative	Total £	Sales tax £	SLCA £	Cash sales £	Discount allowed £

Cash payments book

Date	Details	Cheque no	Code	Total £	Sales tax £	PLCA £	Cash purchases £	Other £	Discounts received £

3 Accounting for receivables

3.1 Sales ledger control account

Within the general ledger the total amount outstanding from receivables is shown in the sales ledger control account. The sales ledger control account may also be referred to as the receivables ledger control account.

The totals of credit sales (from the sales day book), returns from customers (from the sales returns day book) and cash received and discounts (from the analysed cash book) are posted to this account. This account therefore shows the total receivables outstanding. It does not give details about individual customers' balances. This is available in the sales ledger for receivables.

However, as both records are compiled from the same sources, the total balances on the customers' individual accounts should equal the outstanding balance on the control account at any time.

3.2 Double entry system

The double entry system operates as follows.

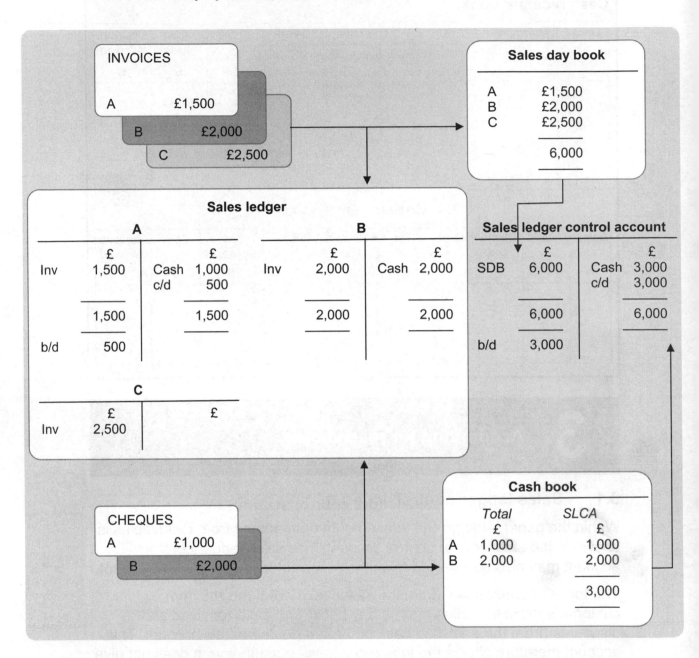

Notice that the remaining balance on the control account (£3,000) is equal to the sum of the remaining balances on the individual receivables' accounts (A £500 + C £2,500).

If all of the accounting entries have been made correctly then the balance on the sales ledger control account should equal the total of the balances on each of the individual receivables' accounts in the sales ledger.

KAPLAN PUBLISHING

3.3 Proforma sales ledger control account

A sales ledger control account normally appears like this.

Sales ledger control account				
	£			£
Balance b/d	X	Returns per sales day book		X
Sales per sales day book	X	* Cash from receivables		X
		* Discounts allowed		X
		Irrecoverable debt written off		X
		Contra entry		X
		Balance c/d		X
	X			X
Balance b/d				
* Per cash receipts book				

Two of these entries, irrecoverable debt and contra entry, are new to you so we will consider them now.

3.4 Irrecoverable debts

Definition

An irrecoverable debt is a debt which is not likely to be received; it is therefore not prudent for the business to consider this debt as an asset.

3.5 Reasons for irrecoverable debts

A business may decide that a debt is irrecoverable (bad) for a number of reasons:

- customer is in liquidation – no cash will be received;
- customer is having difficulty paying although not officially in liquidation;
- customer disputes the debt and refuses to pay all or part of it.

3.6 Accounting for irrecoverable debts

The business must make an adjustment to write off the irrecoverable debt from the customer's account in the sales ledger and to write it off in the general ledger. The double entry in the general ledger is:

DR   Irrecoverable debt expense

   CR   Sales ledger control account

Notice that the irrecoverable debt becomes an expense of the business. Writing off irrecoverable debts decreases the profits made by a business, but is not deducted from sales. The sale was made in the anticipation of receiving the money but, if the debt is not to be received, this does not negate the sale it is just an added expense of the business.

The irrecoverable debt must also be written off in the individual receivable's account in the sales ledger by crediting the customer's account as this amount is not going to be received.

When you invoiced the customer you will have recorded the sales tax and paid it to the tax authorities (HMRC). Once the debt is more than 6 months old and it has been determined that the customer is not going to pay you, you can reclaim that sales tax back from the tax authorities (HMRC).

DR   Irrecoverable debt expense   Net amount

Dr   Sales tax control account   Sales tax amount

   CR   Sales ledger control account   Gross amount

3.7 Contra entries

A further type of adjustment that may be required to sales ledger and purchases ledger control accounts is a contra entry.

3.8 Why a contra entry is required

In some instances a business will be both a receivable and a payable of another business as it both buys from the business and sells to it. If this is the case then there will be money owed to the business and money owing from it. This can be simplified by making an adjustment known as a contra entry.

Example

James Associates has a customer, X Brothers. X Brothers also sells goods to James Associates. Therefore X Brothers is both a receivable and a payable of James Associates. The subsidiary ledger accounts of James Associates show the following position:

Sales ledger – receivables

X Brothers

	£		£
Balance b/d	250		

Purchases ledger – payables

X Brothers

	£		£
		Balance b/d	100

The problem here is that X Brothers owes James Associates £250 and is owed £100 by James Associates. If both parties are in agreement it makes more sense to net these two amounts off and to say that X Brothers owes James Associates just £150. This is achieved in accounting terms by a contra entry.

Solution

Step 1 Take the smaller of the two amounts and debit the purchases ledger account for the payable and credit the sales ledger account for the receivable with this amount.

Sales ledger – receivables

X Brothers

	£		£
Balance b/d	250	Contra	100

Purchases ledger – payables

X Brothers

	£		£
Contra	100	Balance b/d	100

Step 2 Balance off the accounts in the subsidiary ledgers.

Sales ledger – receivables

X Brothers

	£		£
Balance b/d	250	Contra	100
		Balance c/d	150
	———		———
	250		250
	———		———
Balance b/d	150		

Purchases ledger – payables

X Brothers

	£		£
Contra	100	Balance b/d	100
	———		

This now shows that X Brothers owes £150 to James Associates and is owed nothing by James Associates.

Step 3 The double entry must also be carried out in the general ledger accounts. This is:

> DR Purchases ledger control account
>
> CR Sales ledger control account

When a contra entry is made you must remember not just to deal with the entries in the subsidiary ledgers but also to put through the double entry in the general ledger accounts, the sales ledger and purchases ledger control accounts.

3.9 General ledger and sales ledger

We will now return to the relationship between the sales ledger control account in the general ledger and the individual accounts for receivables in the sales ledger.

💡 Example

James has been trading for two months. He has four credit customers. James is not registered for sales tax. Here is the day book for the first two months:

Sales day book (SDB)

Date	Customer	Invoice	£
02.2.X4	Peter Brown	01	50.20
05.2.X4	Ian Smith	02	80.91
07.2.X4	Sid Parsons	03	73.86
23.2.X4	Eva Lane	04	42.30
	Total		247.27
09.3.X4	Ian Smith	05	23.96
15.3.X4	Sid Parsons	06	34.72
20.3.X4	Peter Brown	07	12.60
24.3.X4	Sid Parsons	08	93.25
31.3.X4	Total		164.53

Here is the receipts side of the analysed cash book for March 20X4 (no cash was received from receivables in February).

Cash receipts book (CRB)

Date	Narrative	Total £	Cash sales £	Sales ledger £	Rent £
01.3.X4	Peter Brown	50.20		50.20	
03.3.X4	Clare Jones	63.80	63.80		
04.3.X4	Molly Dell	110.00			110.00
12.3.X4	Sid Parsons	50.00		50.00	
13.3.X4	Emily Boyd	89.33	89.33		
20.3.X4	Frank Field	92.68	92.68		
25.3.X4	Eva Lane	42.30		42.30	
31.3.X4	Total	498.31	245.81	142.50	110.00

We will write up the sales ledger and the sales ledger control account and compare the balances.

Solution

Sales ledger – receivables

Peter Brown

		£			£
02.2.X4	01	50.20	28.2.X4	c/d	50.20
		50.20			50.20
01.3.X4	b/d	50.20	01.3.X4	Cash	50.20
20.3.X4	07	12.60	31.3.X4	c/d	12.60
		62.80			62.80
01.4.X4	b/d	12.60			

Eva Lane

		£			£
23.2.X4	04	42.30	28.2.X4	c/d	42.30
		42.30			42.30
01.3.X4	b/d	42.30	25.3.X4	Cash	42.30

Sid Parsons

		£			£
07.2.X4	03	73.86	28.2.X4	c/d	73.86
		73.86			73.86
01.3.X4	b/d	73.86	12.3.X4	Cash	50.00
15.3.X4	06	34.72	31.3.X4	c/d	151.83
24 3 X4	08	93.25			
		201.83			201.83
01.4.X4	b/d	151.83			

Ian Smith

		£			£
05.2.X4	02	80.91	28.2.X4	c/d	80.91
		80.91			80.91
01.3.X4	b/d	80.91	31.3.X4	c/d	104.87
09.3.X4	05	23.96			
		104.87			104.87
01.4.X4	b/d	104.87			

Sales ledger control account

		£			£
28.2.X4	SDB	247.27	28.2.X4	c/d	247.27
		247.27			247.27
01.3.X4	b/d	247.27	31.3.X4	CRB	142.50
31.3.X4	SDB	164.53	31.3.X4	c/d	269.30
		411.80			411.80
01.4.X4	b/d	269.30			

Let us compare balances at 31 March 20X4.

Subsidiary ledger – receivables

	£
Peter Brown	12.60
Eva Lane	–
Sid Parsons	151.83
Ian Smith	104.87
	269.30
Sales ledger control account	269.30

As the double entry has been correctly carried out, the total of the balances on the individual receivables' accounts in the sales ledger is equal to the balance on the sales ledger control account.

4 Sales ledger control account reconciliation

4.1 Introduction

Comparing the sales ledger control account balance with the total of the sales ledger accounts is a form of internal control. The reconciliation should be performed on a regular basis by the sales ledger clerk and reviewed and approved by an independent person.

If the total of the balances on the sales ledger do not equal the balance on the sales ledger control account then an error or errors have been made in either the general ledger or sales ledger, and these must be discovered and corrected.

4.2 Journal entries

We saw earlier how a journal can be used to enter opening balances to start a new period of accounts. Journal entries are also used for unusual items that do not appear in the primary records, or for the correction of errors or making of adjustments to ledger accounts.

A typical journal entry to write off an irrecoverable debt is shown below:

Sequential journal number

Authorisation

Description of why double entry is necessary

Double entry

Equal totals as journal must balance

JOURNAL ENTRY		No: 0667		
Prepared by:	P Freer			
Authorised by:	P Simms			
Date:	3 October 20X2			
Narrative:				
To write off irrecoverable debt from L C Hamper				
Account	Code	Debit	Credit	
Irrecoverable debts expense	ML28	102.00		
Receivables' control	ML06		102.00	
TOTALS		102.00	102.000	

💡 Example

The total sales for the month were posted from the sales day book as £4,657.98 instead of £4,677.98. This must be corrected using a journal entry.

Solution

The journal entry to correct this error will be as follows:

JOURNAL ENTRY		No: 97		
Prepared by:	A Graimm			
Authorised by:	L R Ridinghood			
Date:	23.7.X3			
Narrative:				
To correct error in posting from SDB				
Account		Code	Debit	Credit
Sales ledger control		ML11	20	
Sales		ML56		20
TOTALS			20	20

The adjustment required is to increase receivables and sales by £20 therefore a debit to sales ledger control and a credit to sales is needed.

4.3 Adjustments in the subsidiary ledger

Adjustments in the subsidiary ledger do not need to be shown in a journal entry. Journal entries are only required for adjustments to the general ledger.

These adjustments should be recorded in memorandum form, with proper authorisation.

4.4   Procedure for a sales ledger control account reconciliation

(1)   The balances on the sales ledger accounts for receivables are extracted, listed and totalled.

(2)   The sales ledger control account is balanced.

(3)   If the two figures differ, then the reasons for the difference must be investigated.

Reasons may include the following:

- An error in the casting of the day book. (The total is posted to the control account whereas the individual invoices are posted to the individual accounts and, therefore, if the total is incorrect, a difference will arise.)

- A transposition error (the figures are switched around, e.g. £87 posted as £78) which could be made in posting either:
    (a)   to the control account (the total figure); or
    (b)   to the individual accounts (the individual transactions).

- A casting error in the cash book column relating to the control account. (The total is posted.)

- A balance omitted from the list of individual accounts.

- A credit balance on an individual account in the sales ledger for receivables which has automatically and wrongly been assumed to be a debit balance.

(4)   Differences which are errors in the control account should be corrected in the control account.

(5)   Differences which are errors in the individual accounts should be corrected by adjusting the list of balances and, of course, the account concerned.

📝 Activity 5

Would the following errors cause a difference to occur between the balance of the sales ledger control account and the total of the balances in the sales ledger?

(a)   The total column of the sales day book was overcast by £100.

(b)   In error H Lambert's account in the sales ledger was debited with £175 instead of M Lambert's account.

(c)   An invoice for £76 was recorded in the sales day book as £67.

Example

The balance on the sales ledger control account for a business at 31 March 20X3 is £14,378.37. The total of the list of sales ledger balances for receivables is £13,935.37.

The difference has been investigated and the following errors have been identified:

- the sales day book was overcast by £1,000;

- a credit note for £150 was entered into an individual receivable's account as an invoice;

- discounts allowed of £143 were correctly accounted for in the sales ledger but were not entered into the general ledger accounts;

- a credit balance on one receivable's account of £200 was mistakenly listed as a debit balance when totalling the individual receivable accounts in the sales ledger.

Prepare the reconciliation between the balance on the sales ledger control account and the total of the individual balances on the sales ledger accounts.

Solution

Step 1 Amend the sales ledger control account for any errors that have been made

Sales ledger control account

	£		£
Balance b/d	14,378.37	SDB overcast	1,000.00
		Discounts allowed	143.00
		Balance c/d	13,235.37
	14,378.37		14,378.37
Balance b/d	13,235.37		

Step 2 Correct the total of the list of balances in the sales ledger.

		£
Original total		13,935.37
Less:	Credit note entered as invoice (2 × 150)	(300.00)
	Credit balance entered as debit balance (2 × 200)	(400.00)
		13,235.37

Activity 6

The balance on Diana's sales ledger control account at 31 December 20X6 was £15,450. The balances on the individual accounts in the sales ledger have been extracted and total £15,705. On investigation the following errors are discovered:

(a) a debit balance of £65 has been omitted from the list of balances;

(b) discounts totalling £70 have been recorded in the individual accounts but not in the control account;

(c) the sales day book was 'overcast' by £200;

(d) a contra entry for £40 has not been entered into the control account; and

(e) an invoice for £180 was recorded correctly in the sales day book but was posted to the receivables' individual account as £810.

Prepare the sales ledger control account reconciliation.

5 Accounting for payables

5.1 Introduction

As we have previously seen, the total amount payable to payables is recorded in the general ledger in the purchases ledger control account. This may also be referred to as the payables ledger control account. The total of credit purchases from the purchases day book, returns to suppliers from the purchases returns day book and the total payments to payables and discounts received taken from the cash payments book are all posted to this account.

The purchases ledger control account shows the total amount that is payable to payables but it does not show the amount owed to individual suppliers. This information is provided by the purchases ledger which contains an account for each individual payable.

Each individual invoice from the purchases day book and each individual credit note from the purchases returns day book is posted to the relevant payable's account in the purchases ledger. Similarly each individual payment to payables and discounts received are posted from the cash payments book to the individual payables' accounts in the purchases ledger.

5.2 Relationship between the purchases ledger control account and the balances in the purchases ledger

The information that is being posted to the purchases ledger control account in total and to the individual accounts in the purchases ledger as individual entries are from the same sources and should in total be the same figures.

Therefore, just as with the sales ledger control account, if the double entry and entries to the purchases ledger have been correctly carried out then the balance on the purchases ledger control account should be equal to the total of the list of balances on the individual payables' accounts in the purchases ledger.

5.3 Proforma purchases ledger control account

A purchases ledger control account normally appears like this.

Purchases ledger control account				
	£			£
Payments to suppliers per analysed cash book		Balance b/d		X
		Purchases per purchases		
Cash	X	day book		X
Discount received	X			
Returns per purchases returns day book	X			
Contra entry	X			
Balance c/d	X			
	X			X
		Balance b/d		X

If all of the accounting entries have been correctly made then the balance on this purchases ledger control account should equal the total of the balances on the individual supplier accounts in the purchases ledger.

6 Purchases ledger control account reconciliation

6.1 Introduction

At each month end the purchases ledger clerk must reconcile the purchases ledger control account and the purchases ledger, just as the sales ledger clerk performed the sales ledger control account reconciliation.

Remember that as well as investigating and discovering the differences, the control account and the individual accounts in the purchases ledger must also be amended for any errors.

6.2 Adjustments to the purchases ledger control account

Any corrections or adjustments made to the purchases ledger control account can be documented as a journal entry.

Example

The total purchases for the month were posted from the purchases day book as £2,547.98 instead of £2,457.98. Prepare a journal to correct this error.

Solution

The journal entry to correct this error will be as follows:

JOURNAL ENTRY		No: 253		
Prepared by:	P Charming			
Authorised by:	U Sister			
Date:	29.8.X5			
Narrative:				
To correct error in posting to payables' control account				
Account		Code	Debit	Credit
Purchase ledger control		GL56	90	
Purchases		GL34		90
TOTALS			90	90

In this case both PLCA and purchases need to be reduced by £90. Therefore a debit to the purchases ledger control and a credit to purchases are required.

6.3 Adjustments in the purchases ledger

Adjustments in the purchases ledger do not need to be documented in a journal entry. Journal entries are only required for adjustments to the general ledger.

Example

The balance on the purchases ledger control account for a business at 30 June was £12,159. The total of the balances on the individual payables' accounts in the purchases ledger was £19,200.

The following errors were also found:

* the cash payments book had been undercast by £20;

* an invoice from Thomas Ltd, a credit supplier, for £2,350 [2,400] was correctly entered in the purchases ledger but had been missed out of the addition of the total in the purchases day book;

* an invoice from Fred Singleton for £2,000 plus sales tax was included in his individual account in the purchases ledger at the net amount;

* an invoice from Horace Shades for £6,000 was entered into the individual account in the purchases ledger twice;

* the same invoice is for £6,000 plus sales tax but the sales tax had not been included in the purchases ledger;

* returns to Horace Shades of £261 had been omitted from the purchases ledger.

You are required to reconcile the purchases ledger control account with the balances on the purchases ledger accounts at 30 June.

Solution

Step 1 Amend the purchases ledger control account to show the correct balance.

Purchases ledger control account

	£		£
Undercast of CPB	20	Balance b/d	12,159
Balance c/d	14,539	Invoice omitted from PDB	2,400
	———		———
	14,559		14,559
	———		———
		Amended balance b/d	14,539

Step 2   Correct the total of the list of purchases ledger balances.

	£
Original total	19,200
Add: Fred Singleton sales tax	400
Less: Horace Shades invoice included twice	(6,000)
Add: Horace Shades sales tax	1,200
Less: Horace Shades returns	(261)
Amended total of list of balances	14,539

Remember that invoices from suppliers should be included in the individual suppliers' accounts in the purchases ledger at the gross amount, including sales tax.

Activity 7

How would each of the following be dealt with in the purchases ledger control account reconciliation?

(a)   A purchase invoice for £36 from P Swift was credited to P Short's account in the subsidiary ledger.

(b)   A purchase invoice for £96 not entered in the purchases day book.

(c)   An undercast of £20 in the total column of the purchases day book.

(d)   A purchase invoice from Short & Long for £42 entered as £24 in the purchases day book.

7   Cause of the difference

You may sometimes be asked you to say what has caused the difference between the control account and the list of balances. If you are asked to do this, the difference will usually be caused by just one error.

An example will illustrate this.

Example

XYZ Ltd has made the following entries in the sales ledger control account.

	£
Opening balance 1 April 20X7	49,139
Credit sales posted from the sales day book	35,000
Discounts allowed	328
Irrecoverable debt written off	127
Cash received from receivables	52,359

The list of balances from the sales ledger totals £31,579.

(a)   Calculate the closing balance on the SLCA at 31 April 2007.

(b)   State one reason for the difference between the SLCA balance and the total of the list of balances.

Solution

(a)   The SLCA

Sales ledger control account

	£		£
Balance b/d	49,139	Discount allowed	328
SDB – sales	35,000	Irrecoverable debt	127
		Cash received	52,359
		Balance c/d	31,325
	84,139		84,139

(b)	Total of sales ledger balances	31,579
	Balance of SLCA at 30 April 20X7	31,325
	Difference	254

Note

You have to look for the fairly obvious clues and also make some assumptions

(i)   It's reasonable to assume that the control account is correct – it may not be, so be careful.

(ii) Calculate the difference and determine whether the list total is larger than the SLCA balance or vice versa.

(iii) See if one of the figures given in the question is the same as the difference or double the difference.

If a figure given is the same as the difference then it is likely that a number has been left out of an account.

If a figure given is double the difference then it is likely that a number has been entered on the wrong side of an account, or possibly entered twice.

- In the above question, the difference is £254.

- The total of the list of ledger balances is bigger than the SLCA balance.

- £254 is not a figure given in the question but the amount £127 is given and the difference is twice this figure.

One possible reason for this is that the irrecoverable debt write off (£127) was entered on the debit side of a ledger account in the sales ledger – that would have made the total of the list £254 larger. Of course there are a million possible reasons – perhaps there was an invoice for £254 and it was entered twice in a sales ledger account – that would have caused the difference, but the assessor is looking for something obvious in the figures given to you – not some speculative reason.

8 Batch control

8.1 Introduction

Throughout this chapter we have been dealing with control accounts in the general ledger and individual receivables and payables accounts in the subsidiary ledgers. We have noted that there will sometimes be a discrepancy between the balance on the control account in the general ledger and the total of the balances in the subsidiary ledgers. Sometimes this difference is caused by correctly entered items that can be reconciled. However, sometimes the difference is caused by an error in the entering of the data. These latter errors can be eliminated or minimised by the use of batch control.

8.2 How a lack of batch control causes problems

Consider the situation where a small business has received 40 cheques from receivables and is going to post these into the accounts for the week. A typical system might be as follows.

(a) John writes the cheques into the total and SLCA columns of the analysed cash received book. John then totals the cash received book for the week and posts the total of the SLCA column to the sales ledger control account. He then writes out the bank paying-in slip and pays the cheques into the bank.

(b) George writes up the individual accounts in the sales ledger from the entries in the main cash book.

The above is a fairly typical system and of course all sorts of things can go wrong.

(a) A cheque could go missing and not be paid into the bank, causing a discrepancy between the entries in the cash book and the bank statement.

(b) John could write the values of one or more of the cheques incorrectly in the cash book, causing the cash book total and the sales ledger control account entry to be incorrect.

(c) George could also write the values of the cheques incorrectly in the sales ledger.

8.3 How batch control helps reduce errors

To improve the system the company employs a system of batch control.

(a) Before the cheques are entered in the cash book, a person unconnected with entering the cheques in the books (Jemima) will total the cheques using a computer spreadsheet such as Excel or an adlisting calculating machine (i.e. a machine which will print out the value of the amounts entered). She will not disclose the total of the cheques.

(b) John will now write the cheques into the cash book and total the cash book as before. He will then compare his total with Jemima's total. If the totals are different, Jemima and John will both check their work until they can agree on a total. This clearly minimises any errors that are likely to be made when entering the cheques in the books of account.

(c) George will write up the sales ledger as before. As a further check, the sales ledger could be passed to another person who would total the entries that George has just made and then compare that total with Jemima's total.

As you can see, by batching the cheques together and producing a total of their value before any entries are made in the books, the company has an excellent check on the accuracy of the entries that are made.

Of course nothing is foolproof. The accountants could enter incorrect amounts in the ledger which compensate for each other thereby still giving the correct total. Alternatively, a cheque might be lost thereby giving an incorrect banking total. But at least the possibility of human error is reduced.

9 · The sales tax control account

Within, Basic Accounting I, we learned about the operation of sales tax to enable us to calculate the amount we would charge on our sales, and the amounts we would reclaim on our purchases. We now need to consider how these transactions would look within the third control account within the general ledger, the sales tax control account, and to appreciate that it is the difference between these two amounts that must be paid to or received from the tax authorities (HMRC).

 Example

The following sales tax figures have been extracted from your day books. Complete the sales tax control account, and find the balance.

Sales day book	22,436
Sales returns day book	674
Purchases day book	15,327

Solution

Sales tax account

Details	Amount £	Details	Amount £
Sales returns (SRDB)	674	Sales (SDB)	22,436
Purchases (PDB)	15,327		
Balance c/d	6,435		
	22,436		**22,436**

The sales tax from the sales daybook is payable to HMRC, whereas the sales tax from the sales returns and the purchases daybooks can be reclaimed. It is the net effect that is payable to HMRC.

Businesses are required to complete a sales tax return, usually on a quarterly basis, to show the amount payable to or reclaimed from the tax authorities (HMRC). Whilst you are not required to complete the return itself, you may be told of the amount showing on the sales tax return and asked to confirm if it agrees to the control account calculated.

Activity 8

The following sales tax figures have been extracted from the books of prime entry.

Sales day book	60,200
Sales returns day book	980
Purchases day book	34,300
Purchases returns day book	2,660
Cash receipts book	112

(a) What will be the entries in the sales tax control account to record the sales tax transactions in the quarter

(b) The sales tax return has been completed and shows an amount owing from the tax authorities of £27,692. Is the sales tax return correct?

Sales tax account

Details	Amount £	Details	Amount £

10 Summary

We started this chapter with a revision of balancing accounts and extended this to entering opening balances in the ledger accounts. Then the chapter moved on to aspects of control and the use of control accounts and control account reconciliations in order to determine the accuracy of the figures in the ledger accounts. The reconciliations, sales ledger and purchases ledger are important and you should ensure that you are happy with the subject matter in this chapter.

Answers to chapter activities

Activity 1

Sales ledger control account

	£		£
SDB – invoices	5,426.23	CRB	3,226.56
		Discounts allowed	315.57
		Balance c/d	1,884.10
	5,426.23		5,426.23
Balance b/d	1,884.10		

Sales tax account

	£		£
PDB	846.72	SDB	1,036.54
Balance c/d	189.82		
	1,036.54		1,036.54
		Balance b/d	189.82

Sales account

	£		£
		SDB	2,667.45
Balance c/d	4,521.37	SDB	1,853.92
	4,521.37		4,521.37
		Balance b/d	4,521.37

Activity 2

(a) Credit balance

(b) Debit balance

(c) Credit balance

(d) Debit balance

Activity 3

Account name	Amount £	Debit / Credit
Bank overdraft	6,975	Credit
Cash	275	Debit
Sales tax payable	2,390	Credit
Motor vehicles	10,500	Debit
Plant and machinery	25,700	Debit
Loan from bank	12,000	Credit
Motor expenses	1,540	Debit
Rent and rates	2,645	Debit
Miscellaneous expenses	725	Debit

Activity 4

Purchases ledger

Bailey Limited

		£			£
01 Dec	Bank	799	01 Dec	Balance b/d	11,750
01 Dec	Discount received	20	01 Dec	Purchases	240
01 Dec	Balance c/d	11,171			
		11,990			11,990
			02 Dec	Balance b/d	11,171

Byng & Company

		£			£
			01 Dec	Balance b/d	1,269
01 Dec	Balance c/d	2,229	01 Dec	Purchases	960
		2,229			2,229
			02 Dec	Balance b/d	2,229

Office Supplies Limited

		£			£
01 Dec	Purchases returns	48	01 Dec	Balance b/d	4,230
01 Dec	Balance c/d	4,518	01 Dec	Purchases	336
		4,566			4,566
			02 Dec	Balance b/d	4,518

O'Connell Frames

		£			£
01 Dec	Purchases returns	2,160	01 Dec	Balance b/d	423
01 Dec	Balance c/d	3,303	01 Dec	Purchases	5,040
		5,463			5,463
			02 Dec	Balance b/d	3,303

General ledger

PLCA

		£			£
01 Dec	Purchases returns	2,208	01 Dec	Balance b/d	82,006
01 Dec	Bank	799	01 Dec	Purchases	6,576
01 Dec	Discounts received	20			
01 Dec	Balance c/d	85,555			
		88,582			88,582
			02 Dec	Balance b/d	85,555

SLCA

		£			£
01 Dec	Balance b/d	180,312	01 Dec	Bank	5,875
01 Dec	Sales	13,440	01 Dec	Balance c/d	187,877
		193,752			193,752
02 Dec	Balance b/d	187,877			

Purchases

		£			£
01 Dec	Balance b/d	90,563			
01 Dec	PLCA	5,200	01 Dec	Balance c/d	95,763
		95,763			95,763
02 Dec	Balance b/d	95,763			

Sales

		£			£
			01 Dec	Balance b/d	301,492
			01 Dec	SLCA	11,200
01 Dec	Balance c/d	313,192	01 Dec	Bank	500
		313,192			313,192
			02 Dec	Balance b/d	313,192

Purchases returns

		£			£
			01 Dec	Balance b/d	306
01 Dec	Balance c/d	2,106	01 Dec	PLCA	1,800
		2,106			2,106
			02 Dec	Balance b/d	2,106

Stationery

	£			£
01 Dec Balance b/d	642	01 Dec PLCA		40
01 Dec PLCA	280	01 Dec Balance c/d		882
	922			922
02 Dec Balance b/d	882			

Discounts received

	£			£
		01 Dec Balance b/d		50
01 Dec Balance c/d	70	01 Dec Payables		20
	70			70
		02 Dec Balance b/d		70

Sales tax

	£			£
01 Dec PLCA	1,096	01 Dec Balance b/d		17,800
		01 Dec PLCA		368
		01 Dec SLCA		2,240
01 Dec Balance c/d	19,412	01 Dec Bank		100
	20,508			20,508
		02 Dec Balance b/d		19,412

Cash receipts book

Date	Narrative	Total	Sales tax	SLCA	Other	Discount
		£	£	£	£	£
20X1						
01 Dec	Lili Chang	600	100		500	
01 Dec	Benley Brothers	5,875		5,875		
		6,475	100	5,875	500	–

Cash payments book

Date	Details	Cheque no	Code	Total £	Sales tax £	PLCA £	Cash purchases £	Other £	Discounts received £
20X1									
01 Dec	Bailey Ltd			799	–	799	–	–	20

	£
Opening balance	3,006
Add: Receipts	6,475
Less:	(799)
Closing balance	8,682

Activity 5

(a) Yes, because the correct detailed entries in the sales day book are posted to the sales ledger accounts and the incorrect total used in the control account.

(b) No, because the arithmetical balance is correct even though the wrong account is used.

(c) No, because the total posted to the SLCA will include the £67 and the entry in the sales ledger will also be for £67. They are both wrong.

Activity 6

- We must first look for those errors which will mean that the sales ledger control account is incorrectly stated. The control account is then adjusted as follows:

Sales ledger control account

	£		£
Balance b/d	15,450	Discounts allowed	70
		Overcast of sales day book	200
		Contra with PLCA	40
		Adjusted balance c/d	15,140
	─────		─────
	15,450		15,450
	─────		─────
Balance b/d	15,140		

- We must then look for errors in the total of the individual balances per the sales ledger. The extracted list of balances must be adjusted as follows:

	£
Original total of list of balances	15,705
Debit balance omitted	65
Transposition error (810 – 180)	(630)
	─────
	15,140
	─────

- As can be seen, the adjusted total of the list of balances now agrees with the balance per the control account.

Activity 7

(a) This does not affect the reconciliation. A correction would simply be made in the subsidiary ledger.

(b) This must be adjusted for in the purchase ledger control account and in the purchases ledger.

(c) This is just an adjustment to the purchase ledger control account.

(d) This will require alteration in both the control account and the purchases ledger.

Activity 8

(a) **Sales tax account**

Details	Amount £	Details	Amount £
Sales Returns (SRDB)	980	Sales (SDB)	60,200
Purchases (PDB)	34,300	Purchases returns (PRDB)	2,660
Balance c/d	27,692	Cash sales (CRB)	112
	62,972		**62,972**

(b) No. The amount of £27,692 is payable to the tax authorities.

11 Test your knowledge

Workbook Activity 9

Record the journal entries needed in the accounts in the general ledger to deal with the opening entries listed below:

Account name	Amount £	Dr ✓	Cr ✓
Cash	2,350		
Capital	20,360		
Motor Vehicles	6,500		
Electricity	800		
Office expenses	560		
Loan from bank	15,000		
Cash at bank	6,400		
Factory equipment	14,230		
Rent	2,500		
Insurance	1,000		
Miscellaneous expenses	1,020		

Workbook Activity 10

The following totals are taken from the books of a business:

	£
Credit balance on purchases ledger control account	5,926
Debit balance on sales ledger control account	10,268
Credit sales	71,504
Credit purchases	47,713
Cash received from credit customers	69,872
Cash paid to payables	47,028
Sales ledger balances written off as bad	96
Sales returns	358
Purchases returns	202
Discounts allowed	1,435
Discounts received	867
Contra entry	75

Required:

(a) Prepare the purchases ledger control account and balance at the end of the month.

(b) Prepare the sales ledger control account and balance at the end of the month.

Workbook Activity 11

The balance on the sales ledger control account of Robin & Co on 30 September 20X0 amounted to £3,825 which did not agree with the net total of the list of sales ledger balances at that date of £3,362.

The errors discovered were as follows:

1   Debit balances in the sales ledger, amounting to £103, had been omitted from the list of balances.

2   An irrecoverable debt amounting to £400 had been written off in the sales ledger but had not been posted to the irrecoverable debts expense account or entered in the control accounts.

3   An item of goods sold to Sparrow, £250, had been entered once in the sales day book but posted to his account twice.

4   No entry had been made in the control account in respect of the transfer of a debit of £70 from Quail's account in the sales ledger to his account in the purchases ledger (a contra entry).

5   The discount allowed column in the cash account had been undercast by £140.

Required:

(a)   Make the necessary adjustments in the sales ledger control account and bring down the balance.

(b)   Show the adjustments to the net total of the original list of balances to reconcile with the amended balance on the sales ledger control account.

Workbook Activity 12

When carrying out the purchases ledger control account reconciliation the following errors were discovered:

(a)   the purchases day book was overcast by £1,000;

(b)   the total of the discount received column in the cash payments book was posted to the general ledger as £89 instead of £98;

(c)   a contra entry of £300 had been entered in the subsidiary ledger but not in the general ledger.

Required:

Produce journal entries to correct each of these errors.

Workbook Activity 13

(a) Show whether each entry will be a debit or credit in the Sales ledger control account in the general ledger.

Details	Amount £	Dr ✓	Cr ✓
Balance of receivables at 1 July	60,580		
Goods sold on credit	18,950		
Payments received from credit customers	20,630		
Discounts allowed	850		
Irrecoverable debt written off	2,400		
Goods returned from credit customers	3,640		

(b) The following debit balances were in the sales ledger on 1 August:

	Amount £
Rock 'n Roll Ltd	10,700
Cavern Ltd	18,420
Tunnel Plc	2,400
Studio 51 Ltd	7,680
Hacienda Ltd	9,955
Warehouse Company	5,255

Required:

Calculate the balance brought down on the sales ledger control account on 1 August using the information from part (a). Then reconcile the balances shown above with the sales ledger control account balance.

	Amount £
Sales ledger control account balance as at 31 July	
Total of sales ledger accounts as at 31 July	
Difference	

(c) What may have caused the difference calculated above?

	✓
Goods returned may have been omitted from the sales ledger	
Irrecoverable debt written off may have been omitted from the sales ledger	
Goods returned may have been entered twice in the sales ledger	
Irrecoverable debt written off may have been entered twice in the sales ledger	

Workbook Activity 14

(a) Show whether each entry will be a debit or credit in the Purchases ledger control account in the general ledger.

Details	Amount £	Dr ✓	Cr ✓
Balance of payables at 1 July	58,420		
Goods bought on credit	17,650		
Payments made to credit suppliers	19,520		
Discounts received	852		
Contra entry with sales ledger control	600		
Goods returned to credit suppliers	570		

(b) The following credit balances were in the purchases ledger on 1 August:

	Amount £
Price & Co	9,570
Andre Ltd	12,478
Hayes Plc	6,895
Lucas Ltd	7,950
Millers & Co	8,546
Griffiths Ltd	7,560

Required:

Calculate the balance brought down on the purchases ledger control account on 1 August using the information from part (a). Then reconcile the balances shown above with the purchases ledger control account balance.

	Amount £
Purchases ledger control account balance as at 31 July	
Total of purchase ledger accounts as at 31 July	
Difference	

(c) What may have caused the difference calculated above?

	✓
Payments made to suppliers may have been understated in the purchase ledger	
Goods returned to suppliers may have been overstated in the purchase ledger	
Goods bought on credit may have been overstated in the purchase ledger	
Contra entry may have been omitted from the purchase ledger	

Suspense accounts and errors

4

Introduction

When preparing a trial balance it may be necessary to open a suspense account to deal with any errors or omissions. The suspense account cannot be allowed to remain permanently in the trial balance, and must be cleared by correcting each of the errors that have caused the trial balance not to balance.

SKILLS

2.1 Identify and record journal entries in the general ledger to correct errors not disclosed by the trial balance

2.2 Identify the types of errors in a bookkeeping system that are not disclosed by extracting a trial balance

2.3 Identify the types of errors in a bookkeeping system that are disclosed by extracting a trial balance:

– addition errors in individual ledger accounts

– single entry transactions

– recording two debits or two credits for a transaction

– errors transferring balances from the general ledger to the trial balance

– omission of a general ledger account

2.4 Re-draft a trial balance following the correction of errors

3.1 Balance a trial balance by recording the difference in a suspense account

CONTENTS

1 The trial balance
2 Opening a suspense account
3 Clearing the suspense account
4 Re-drafting the trial balance

3.2 Prepare journal entries to correct bookkeeping errors and clear the balance on the suspense account

3.3 Record the journal entries in the general ledger to clear the suspense account

3.4 Re-draft a trial balance following the correction of errors and the elimination of a suspense account

KAPLAN PUBLISHING

1 The trial balance

1.1 Introduction

We saw in Basic Accounting I that one of the purposes of the trial balance is to provide a check on the accuracy of the double entry bookkeeping. If the trial balance does not balance then an error or a number of errors have occurred and this must be investigated and the errors corrected.

1.2 Errors detected by the trial balance

The following types of error will cause a difference in the trial balance and therefore will be detected by the trial balance and can be investigated and corrected:

A single entry – if only one side of a double entry has been made then this means that the trial balance will not balance e.g. if only the debit entry for receipts from receivables has been made then the debit total on the trial balance will exceed the credit balance.

A casting error – if a ledger account has not been balanced correctly due to a casting error then this will mean that the trial balance will not balance.

A transposition error – if an amount in a ledger account or a balance on a ledger account has been transposed and incorrectly recorded then the trial balance will not balance e.g. a debit entry was recorded correctly as £5,276 but the related credit entry was entered as £5,726.

An extraction error – if a ledger account balance is incorrectly recorded on the trial balance either by recording the wrong figure or putting the balance on the wrong side of the trial balance then the trial balance will not balance.

An omission error – if a ledger account balance is inadvertently omitted from the trial balance then the trial balance will not balance.

Two entries on one side – instead of a debit and credit entry if a transaction is entered as a debit in two accounts or as a credit in two accounts then the trial balance will not balance.

1.3 Errors not detected by the trial balance

A number of types of errors however will not cause the trial balance not to balance and therefore cannot be detected by preparing a trial balance:

An error of original entry – this is where the wrong figure is entered as both the debit and credit entry e.g. a payment of the electricity expense was correctly recorded as a debit in the electricity account and a credit to the bank account but it was recorded as £300 instead of £330.

A compensating error – this is where two separate errors are made, one on the debit side of the accounts and the other on the credit side, and by coincidence the two errors are of the same amount and therefore cancel each other out.

An error of omission – this is where an entire double entry is omitted from the ledger accounts. As both the debit and credit have been omitted the trial balance will still balance.

An error of commission – with this type of error a debit entry and an equal credit entry have been made but one of the entries has been to the wrong account e.g. if the electricity expense was debited to the rent account but the credit entry was correctly made in the bank account – here both the electricity account and rent account will be incorrect but the trial balance will still balance.

An error of principle – this is similar to an error of commission but the entry has been made in the wrong type of account e.g. if the electricity expense was debited to a non-current asset account – again both the electricity account and the non-current asset account would be incorrect but the trial balance would still balance.

It is important that a trial balance is prepared on a regular basis in order to check on the accuracy of the double entry. However not all errors in the accounting system can be found by preparing a trial balance.

1.4 Correction of errors

Errors will normally be corrected by putting through a journal entry for the correction.

The procedure for correcting errors is as follows:

Step 1

Determine the precise nature of the incorrect double entry that has been made.

Step 2

Determine the correct entries that should have been made.

Step 3

Produce a journal entry that cancels the incorrect part and puts through the correct entries.

KAPLAN PUBLISHING

Example

The electricity expense of £450 has been correctly credited to the bank account but has been debited to the rent account.

Step 1

The incorrect entry has been to debit the rent account with £450

Step 2

The correct entry is to debit the electricity account with £450

Step 3

The journal entry required is:

DR   Electricity account   £450

CR   Rent account   £450

Note that this removes the incorrect debit from the rent account and puts the correct debit into the electricity account.

Activity 1

Colin returned some goods to a supplier because they were faulty. The original purchase price of these goods was £8,260.

The ledger clerk has correctly treated the double entry but used the figure £8,620.

What is the correcting entry which needs to be made?

2 Opening a suspense account

2.1   Introduction

A suspense account is used as a temporary account to deal with errors and omissions. It means that it is possible to continue with the production of financial accounts whilst the reasons for any errors are investigated and then corrected.

2.2 Reasons for opening a suspense account

A suspense account will be opened in two main circumstances:

(a) the bookkeeper does not know how to deal with one side of a transaction;

or

(b) the trial balance does not balance.

2.3 Unknown entry

In some circumstances the bookkeeper may come across a transaction for which he is not certain of the correct double entry and therefore rather than making an error, one side of the entry will be put into a suspense account until the correct entry can be determined.

Example

A new bookkeeper is dealing with a cheque received from a garage for £800 for the sale of an old car. He correctly debits the bank account with the amount of the cheque but does not know what to do with the credit entry.

Solution

He will enter it in the suspense account:

Suspense account

	£		£
		Bank account – receipt from sale of car	800

2.4 Trial balance does not balance

If the total of the debits on the trial balance does not equal the total of the credits then an error or a number of errors have been made. These must be investigated, identified and eventually corrected. In the meantime the difference between the debit total and the credit total is inserted as a suspense account balance in order to make the two totals agree.

Example

The totals of the trial balance are as follows:

	Debits £	Credits £
Totals as initially extracted	108,367	109,444
Suspense account, to make the TB balance	1,077	
	109,444	109,444

Suspense

	£		£
Opening balance	1,077		

Activity 2

The debit balances on a trial balance exceed the credit balances by £2,600. Open up a suspense account to record this difference.

3 Clearing the suspense account

3.1 Introduction

Whatever the reason for the suspense account being opened it is only ever a temporary account. The reasons for the difference must be identified and then correcting entries should be put through the ledger accounts, via the journal, in order to correct the accounts and clear the suspense account balance to zero.

3.2 Procedure for clearing the suspense account

Step 1

Determine the incorrect entry that has been made or the omission from the ledger accounts.

Step 2

Determine the journal entry required to correct the error or omission – this will not always mean that an entry is required in the suspense account e.g. when the electricity expense was debited to the rent account the journal entry did not require any entry to be made in the suspense account.

Step 3

If there is an entry to be made in the suspense account put this into the suspense account – when all the corrections have been made the suspense account should normally have no remaining balance on it.

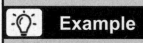 **Example**

A trial balance has been extracted and did not balance. The debit column totalled £200,139 and the credit column totalled £200,239.

You discover the cash purchases £100 have been correctly entered into the cash account but no entry has been made in the purchases account.

Draft a journal entry to correct this error, and complete the suspense ledger account.

Solution

As the debit entries and credit entries do not match, we will be required to open up a suspense account to hold this difference until we can correct it.

Suspense

Detail	Amount £	Detail	Amount £
TB	100	Journal 1 (detailed below)	100
	100		**100**

A debit entry is required in the purchases account and the credit is to the suspense account.

		£	£
Dr	Purchases account	100	
Cr	Suspense account		100

Being correction of double entry for cash purchases.

Remember that normally a journal entry needs a narrative to explain what it is for – however in some assessments you are told not to provide the narratives so always read the requirements carefully.

Example

On 31 December 20X0 the trial balance of John Jones, a small manufacturer, failed to agree and the difference of £967 was entered as a debit balance on the suspense account. After the final accounts had been prepared the following errors were discovered and the difference was eliminated.

(1) A purchase of goods from A Smith for £170 had been credited in error to the account of H Smith.

(2) The purchase day book was undercast by £200.

(3) Machinery purchased for £150 had been debited to the purchases account.

(4) Discounts received of £130 had been posted to the debit of the discounts received account.

(5) Rates paid by cheque £46 had been posted to the debit of the rates account as £64.

(6) Cash drawings by the owner of £45 had been entered in the cash account correctly but not posted to the drawings account.

(7) A non-current asset balance of £1,200 had been omitted from the trial balance.

Required:

(a) Show the journal entries necessary to correct the above errors.

(b) Show the entries in the suspense account to eliminate the differences entered in the suspense account.

Note: The control accounts are part of the double-entry.

Solution

(Note that not all the errors relate to the suspense account. Part of the way of dealing with these questions is to identify which entries do not relate to the suspense account. Do not assume that they all do just because this is a question about suspense accounts.)

Journal – John Jones

		Dr £	Cr £
31 December 20X0			
1	H Smith	170	
	A Smith		170
	Being adjustment of incorrect entry for purchases from A Smith - this correction takes place in the purchases ledger (no effect on suspense account)		
2	Purchases	200	
	Purchases ledger control account		200
	Being correction of undercast of purchases day book (no effect on suspense account as control account is the double entry. However the error should have been found during the reconciliation of the control account.)		
3	Machinery	150	
	Purchases		150
	Being adjustment for wrong entry for machinery purchased (no effect on suspense account)		
4	Suspense account	260	
	Discount received		260
	Being correction of discounts entered on wrong side of account		
5	Suspense account	18	
	Rates		18
	Being correction of transposition error to rates account		
6	Drawings	45	
	Suspense account		45
	Being completion of double entry for drawings		
7	Non-current asset	1,200	
	Suspense account		1,200
	Being inclusion of non-current asset balance. There is no double entry for this error in the ledger as the mistake was to omit the item from the trial balance		

Suspense account

	£		£
Difference in trial balance	967	Drawings	45
Discounts received	260	Non-current asset per trial balance	1,200
Rates	18		
	1,245		1,245

Make sure you realise that not all error corrections will require any entry to the suspense account

Activity 3

GA extracted the following trial balance from his ledgers at 31 May 20X4.

	£	£
Petty cash	20	
Capital		1,596
Drawings	1,400	
Sales		20,607
Purchases	15,486	
Purchases returns		210
Inventory (1 January 20X4)	2,107	
Fixtures and fittings	710	
Sales ledger control	1,819	
Purchases ledger control		2,078
Carriage on purchases	109	
Carriage on sales	184	
Rent and rates	460	
Light and heat	75	
Postage and telephone	91	
Sundry expenses	190	
Cash at bank	1,804	
	24,455	24,491

The trial balance did not agree. On investigation, GA discovered the following errors which had occurred during the month of May.

(1)   In extracting the receivables balance the credit side of the sales ledger control account had been overcast by £10.

(2)   An amount of £4 for carriage on sales had been posted in error to the carriage on purchases account.

(3)   A credit note for £17 received from a payable had been entered in the purchase returns account but no entry had been made in the purchases ledger control account.

(4)   £35 charged by Builders Ltd for repairs to GA's private residence had been charged, in error, to the sundry expenses account.

(5)   A payment of a telephone bill of £21 had been entered correctly in the cash book but had been posted, in error, to the postage and telephone account as £12.

Required:

State what corrections you would make in GA's ledger accounts (using journal entries) and re-write the trial balance as it should appear after all the above corrections have been made. Show how the suspense account is cleared.

4   Re-drafting the trial balance

Once the suspense account has been cleared, it is important to re-draft the trial balance to ensure that the debit column and credit column agree.

Example

On 30 November an initial trial balance was extracted which did not balance, and a suspense account was opened. On 1 December journal entries were prepared to correct the errors that had been found, and clear the suspense account. The list of balances and the journal entries are shown below.

Re-draft the trial balance by placing the figures in the debit or credit column, after taking into account the journal entries which will clear suspense.

	Balances as at 30 November	Balances as at 1 December	
		Debit £	Credit £
Motor vehicles	10,500		
Inventory	2,497		
Bank overdraft	1,495		
Petty cash	162		
Sales ledger control	6,811		
Purchases ledger control	2,104		
Sales tax owing to tax authorities	1,329		
Capital	15,000		
Sales	47,036		
Purchases	27,914		
Purchase returns	558		
Wages	12,000		
Motor expenses	947		
Drawings	6,200		
Suspense (debit balance)	491		

Journals

Account	Debit £	Credit £
Motor expenses		9
Suspense	9	
Being to correct transposition error when recording expense		

Account	Debit £	Credit £
Drawings	500	
Suspense		500
Being to correctly analyse unknown cheque payment.		

Solution

	Balances as at 30 November	Balances as at 1 December	
		Debit £	Credit £
Motor vehicles	10,500	10,500	
Inventory	2,497	2,497	
Bank overdraft	1,495		1,495
Petty cash	162	162	
Sales ledger control	6,811	6,811	
Purchases ledger control	2,104		2,104
Sales tax owing to tax authorities	1,329		1,329
Capital	15,000		15,000
Sales	47,036		47,036
Purchases	27,914	27,914	
Purchase returns	558		558
Wages	12,000	12,000	
Motor expenses	947	**938**	
Drawings	6,200	**6,700**	
Suspense (debit balance)	491		
		67,522	67,588

67,522

The drawings and the motor expenses figures have been amended for the journals and the trial balance columns agree without the need for a suspense account.

5 Summary

Preparation of the trial balance is an important element of control over the double entry system but it will not detect all errors. The trial balance will still balance if a number of types of error are made. If the trial balance does not balance then a suspense account will be opened temporarily to make the debits equal the credits in the trial balance. The errors or omissions that have caused the difference on the trial balance must be discovered and then corrected using journal entries. Not all errors will require an entry to the suspense account. However, any that do should be put through the suspense account in order to try to eliminate the balance on the account.

Answers to chapter activities

Activity 1

Step 1

The purchases ledger control account has been debited and the purchases returns account credited but with £8,620 rather than £8,260.

Step 2

Both of the entries need to be reduced by the difference between the amount used and the correct amount (8,620 – 8,260) = £360

Step 3

Journal entry:	£	£
Dr Purchases returns account	360	
Cr Purchases ledger control account		360

Being correction of misposting of purchases returns.

Activity 2

As the debit balances exceed the credit balances the balance needed is a credit balance to make the two totals equal.

Suspense account

	£		£
		Opening balance	2,600

Activity 3

			Dr £	Cr £
1	Debit	Sales ledger control account	10	
	Credit	Suspense account		10
	being correction of undercast in sales ledger control account			
2	Debit	Carriage on sales	4	
	Credit	Carriage on purchases		4
	being correction of wrong posting			
3	Debit	Purchases ledger control account	17	
	Credit	Suspense account		17
	being correction of omitted entry			
4	Debit	Drawings	35	
	Credit	Sundry expenses		35
	being payment for private expenses			
5	Debit	Postage and telephone	9	
	Credit	Suspense account		9
	being correction of transposition error			

Suspense account

	£		£
Difference per trial balance (24,455 – 24,491)	36	SLCA	10
		PLCA	17
		Postage	9
	36		36

Trial balance after adjustments

	Dr £	Cr £
Petty cash	20	
Capital		1,596
Drawings	1,435	
Sales		20,607
Purchases	15,486	
Purchases returns		210
Inventory at 1 January 20X4	2,107	
Fixtures and fittings	710	
Sales ledger control account	1,829	
Purchases ledger control account		2,061
Carriage on purchases	105	
Carriage on sales	188	
Rent and rates	460	
Light and heat	75	
Postage and telephone	100	
Sundry expenses	155	
Cash at bank	1,804	
	24,474	24,474

6 Test your knowledge

Workbook Activity 4

Which of the errors below are, or are not, disclosed by the trial balance?
(Ignore sales tax in all cases)

(a)   Recording a receipt from a receivable in the bank account only.

(b)   Recording bank payment of £56 for motor expenses as £65 in the expense account.

(c)   Recording a credit purchase on the debit side of the purchase ledger control account and the credit side of the purchases account.

(d)   Recording a payment for electricity in the insurance account.

(e)   Recording a bank receipt for cash sales on the credit side of both the bank and the sales account.

(f)   Incorrectly calculating the balance on the motor vehicles account.

(g)   Writing off an irrecoverable debt in the irrecoverable debt expense and sales ledger control accounts only.

(h)   An account with a ledger balance of £3500 was recorded on the Trial Balance as £350.

Workbook Activity 5

Luxury Caravans Ltd's initial trial balance includes a suspense account with a balance of £2,800 as shown below:

	£
Receivables	33,440
Bank (debit balance)	2,800
Sales	401,300
Inventory	24,300
Wages	88,400
Telephone	2,200
Motor car	12,000
Sales tax (credit balance)	5,300
Electricity	3,800
Rent	16,200
Purchases	241,180
Purchases returns	1,600
Sales returns	4,200
Office equipment	5,000
Capital	49,160
Motor expenses	5,040
Discounts allowed	4,010
Discounts received	2,410
Payables	20,000
Drawings	40,000
Suspense (credit balance)	2,800

The following errors have been discovered:

- Rent of £200 has been debited to the motor expenses account

- An electricity payment of £800 has been debited to both the electricity and the bank account

- The balance on the discounts received account has been incorrectly extracted to the TB – the actual balance on the ledger account was £4210

- The balance on the miscellaneous expenses account of £500 was omitted from the TB

- The purchase returns day book for 22 May was incorrectly totalled, as shown below:

Purchase returns day book					
Date	Details	Credit note number	Total £	Sales tax £	Net £
22 May	Todd Ltd	578	4,320	720	3,600
22 May	Fallon Ltd	579	720	120	600
22 May	Dean's Plc	580	960	160	800
	Totals		6,000	1,100	5,000

Required:

(a)   Produce journal entries to correct all of the errors above.

(b)   Re-draft the trial balance using the balances above and your journal entries to show the suspense account has been cleared.

Payroll procedures

5

Introduction

We have previously seen how payments by cheque and other methods are made from the bank account for purchases and expenses. In this chapter we will consider one of the most significant payments that most businesses will make either weekly or monthly – wages and salaries.

KNOWLEDGE

5.3 Give examples of the types of transactions that might be entered into the bookkeeping system by using the journal

– wages/salaries

– PAYE/NIC liability

SKILLS

4.3 Prepare and enter the journal entries in the general ledger to process payroll transactions

CONTENTS

1 Overview of the payroll function
2 Gross pay
3 Income tax
4 National Insurance contributions
5 Other deductions
6 Payroll accounting procedures

1 Overview of the payroll function

1.1 Introduction

The payroll system in a business is one of the most important. The payroll staff not only have a responsibility to calculate correctly the amount of pay due to each employee but they must also ensure that each employee is paid on time with the correct amount and that amounts due to external parties such as HM Revenue and Customs are correctly determined and paid on time.

There are many facets to the payroll function and each will be briefly covered as an introduction in this section and then considered in more detail in later sections of the chapter.

1.2 Calculation of gross pay

The initial calculation that must be carried out for each employee is the calculation of the employee's gross pay. Gross pay is the wage or salary due to the employee for the amount of work done in the period which may be a week or a month depending upon how frequently the employees are paid.

Gross pay may depend upon a number of factors:

- basic hours worked;
- overtime hours worked;
- bonus;
- commission;
- holiday pay;
- sick pay.

1.3 Deductions

Once the gross pay for each employee has been determined then a number of deductions from this amount will be made to arrive at the net pay for the employee. Net pay is the amount that the employee will actually receive.

Some deductions are compulsory or statutory:

- Income tax in the form of PAYE;
- National Insurance Contributions (NIC) which can also be referred to as social security payments.

Other deductions are at the choice of the employer or employee and are therefore non-statutory:

- Save as you earn;

- Give as you earn;

- Pension contributions.

1.4 Payment of wages or salaries

Once the net pay has been determined then each employee must be paid the correct amount, by the most appropriate method at the correct time.

1.5 Payments to external agencies

As you will see later in the chapter employers deduct income tax and NIC from each employee's wages or salaries and the employer must also pay its own NIC contribution for each employee. This is done by making payment to HM Revenue and Customs on a regular basis and this is therefore another responsibility of the payroll function.

1.6 Accounting for wages and salaries

Finally once the wages and salaries for the period have been paid then the amounts involved must be correctly entered into the ledger accounts.

1.7 Accuracy and confidentiality

Whilst carrying out all of these calculations and functions it is obviously important that the calculations are made with total accuracy. Not only is the amount that each individual will be paid dependent upon these calculations but there is a statutory duty to make the correct deductions from gross pay and to pay these over to HM Revenue and Customs.

Payroll staff deal with confidential and sensitive information about individuals such as the rate of pay for an individual. It is of the utmost importance that such details are kept confidential and are not made public nor allowed to be accessed by unauthorised personnel.

2 Gross pay

2.1 Introduction

Gross pay is the total amount payable to the employee before any deductions have been made. Gross pay can be made up of many different elements, e.g.

- normal wages or salary;
- overtime;
- shift payments;
- bonus;
- commission;
- holiday pay;
- statutory sick pay (or SSP); and
- statutory maternity pay (or SMP).

2.2 Wages and salaries

These are fairly straightforward. Employees will have an agreed monthly, weekly or hourly rate.

The monthly and weekly rates will not need any further calculations.

However, for hourly paid employees calculations will be needed for the total earnings. The source of this information might be clock cards.

Q Definition

A clock card is a card which records the hours worked by an employee.

As the employee arrives or leaves they put their card in the slot of a special clock. The mechanism inside the clock stamps the time on the card.

The payroll clerk would transfer the number of hours worked onto special calculation sheets.

2.3　Overtime and shift payments

These need to be identified so that the payroll clerk can calculate the amount payable.

Overtime is hours worked which are over and above the agreed number of weekly or monthly hours for that employee. For example, it may be agreed that an employee has a standard working week of 38 hours. If he works for 42 hours in a week then he has worked 4 hours of overtime.

Overtime or shifts worked might be recorded on:

- clock cards;

- timesheets; or

- authorisation forms (signed by the employee's supervisor).

Some employees are paid at a higher rate for overtime. They might be paid at one and a half times the normal rate. This is called time and a half.

Twice the normal rate is double time.

Some employees might be paid premium rates or bonuses for working certain shifts.

2.4　Bonus and commission payments

The business may pay certain employees a bonus. This bonus may be for achieving a particular target.

Company directors often receive a bonus if the company achieves certain profits.

Companies with a large number of sales representatives may pay their sales representatives a commission as part of their salary. This commission is based on the value of the sales they make.

For instance, a salesman might be paid a basic salary of £10,000 a year plus a 1% commission on sales that he makes.

2.5　Holiday pay

Most employers pay their employees even while they are on holiday.

If the employee is paid monthly, then there is no problem. The employee is paid the usual amount at the normal time.

If the employee is paid weekly, they would prefer to be paid for the holiday period in advance. This means that if the employee is taking two weeks' holiday they will have to be paid three weeks' wages at once.

2.6 Statutory sick pay (SSP) and statutory maternity pay (SMP)

For basic accounting you will really only need to be concerned about basic wages and salaries, overtime and bonus payments.

If there is a reference to SSP or SMP you will be told how to deal with it.

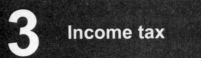

3 Income tax

3.1 Introduction

Everybody in the UK has a potential liability to pay tax on their income.

Individuals pay **income tax**. The rate of tax depends on the amount of their income.

> **Q Definition**
>
> Income tax is a tax on individuals' income.

3.2 Tax-free income

Everybody is entitled to some tax-free income.

This tax-free sum is known as the personal allowance.

> **Q Definition**
>
> The personal allowance is an amount which an individual is allowed to earn tax-free.

3.3 How income tax is paid

Employees in the UK pay their income tax through the **PAYE** (or Pay As You Earn) **scheme**.

> **Q Definition**
>
> The PAYE scheme is a national scheme whereby employers withhold tax and other deductions from their employees' wages and salaries when they are paid. The deductions are then paid over monthly to HM Revenue and Customs by the employer.

Looking at tax alone, the main advantages of this scheme are:

- employees pay the tax as they earn the income;

- most people do not have to complete a tax return unless they have several different sources of income;

- employers act as unpaid tax collectors (this is a serious responsibility and they can be fined for mistakes); and

- the government receives a steady stream of revenue throughout the year.

Activity 1

Under the PAYE Scheme who pays over the income tax to the Collector of Taxes?

A   The employee

B   The employer

C   The government

D   The Inspector of Taxes

---

4   National Insurance contributions

4.1   What is National Insurance?

National Insurance is a state scheme which pays certain benefits including:

- retirement pensions;

- widow's allowances and pensions;

- jobseeker's allowance;

- incapacity benefit; and

- maternity allowance.

The scheme is run by HM Revenue and Customs.

The scheme is funded by people who are currently in employment.

Most people in employment (including partners in partnerships, and sole traders) who have earnings above a certain level must pay National Insurance contributions.

4.2 Types of National Insurance contributions

Both the employer and the employee pay National Insurance contributions.

(a) **Employees' National Insurance contributions**

The employer deducts National Insurance contributions from an employee's weekly wage or monthly salary, and pays these to HM Revenue and Customs. Income tax and National Insurance contributions are both taxes on income, but they have different historical origins and are calculated in different ways. Employees' National Insurance is now, however, similar to income tax in many respects, and is really a form of income tax with another name.

Like income tax, employees' NI contributions are deducted from pay. The amount of the contributions an employee pays is linked to his or her earnings, and is obtained by reference to National Insurance tables supplied by HM Revenue and Customs.

You are not required to know how to use NI tables.

(b) **Employer's National Insurance contributions**

In addition to deducting employees' National Insurance contributions from each employee's wages or salary, an employer is required to pay the employer's National Insurance contributions for each employee. The amount payable for each employee is linked to the size of his or her earnings.

Employer's National Insurance contributions are therefore an employment tax. They are not deducted from the employee's gross pay. They are an additional cost of payroll to the employer, paid for by the employer rather than the employee.

5 Other deductions

5.1 Statutory deductions

So far we have looked at two types of deductions which the employer has to make from their employee's gross pay **by law**. These are **income tax** and **National Insurance** contributions. These are statutory deductions.

5.2 Non-statutory deductions

The employee may also choose to have further deductions made from their gross pay. These include:

- superannuation (pension) payments.

- payments under the **save as you earn scheme**; this is a strictly governed scheme offered by some employers that allows you to save a regular amount each pay day. You would use this money to buy shares in the company at a later date.

- payments under the **give as you earn scheme**; this scheme allows employees to request that their employer withhold a certain amount from their salary and pay it over to a charity, on their behalf.

- other payments, e.g. subscriptions to sports and social clubs and trade unions.

5.3 Summary of deductions and payments

It is time to summarise what deductions the employer makes from the employee's gross salary, and to whom the employer makes the various payments.

To process the payroll an employer must, **for each employee**:

- calculate the gross wage or salary for the period;

- calculate the income tax payable out of these earnings;

- calculate the employee's National Insurance contributions that are deductible;

- calculate any non-statutory deductions;

- calculate the employer's National Insurance contributions.

The employer must then:

- make the payment of net pay to each employee;

- make the payments of all the non-statutory deductions from pay to the appropriate other organisations;

- pay the employee's PAYE, the employee's NIC and the employer's NIC to HM Revenue and Customs for all employees.

Example

John earns £12,000 per annum. His PAYE, NIC and other deductions and the employer's NIC for the month of May 20X4 are:

	£
PAYE	125
Employee's NIC	80
Contribution to personal pension scheme	50
Employer's NIC	85

Calculate:

(a)   John's net pay;

(b)   the cost to the employer of employing John;

(c)   the amounts to be paid to the various organisations involved.

Solution

			Paid by employer to:
Gross pay per month		1,000	
Less: PAYE	125		HMRC
Employee's NIC	80		HMRC
Personal pension	50		Pension company
		(255)	
Net pay		745	John
Employer's NIC	85		HMRC

(a)   John's net pay is £745.

(b)   The cost of employing John is (1,000 + 85) = £1,085.

(c)   The pension company is paid £50 by the employer.

HM Revenue and Customs is paid £290 by the employer:

	£
PAYE	125
Employee's NIC	80
Employer's NIC	85
	290

Where there are many employees, the employer will pay the amounts calculated per (c) above for all employees to HM Revenue and Customs with one cheque.

6 Payroll accounting procedures

6.1 Introduction

The accounting for wages and salaries is based upon two fundamental principles:

- the accounts must reflect the full cost to the employer of employing someone (which is their gross pay plus the employer's NI contribution);

- the accounts must show the payable for PAYE and NIC that must be paid over to HM Revenue and Customs on a regular basis, usually monthly.

We therefore need two accounts, plus a third control account.

(a) The wages expense account which shows the full cost of employing the staff.

(b) The PAYE/NIC account which shows the amount to be paid to HM Revenue and Customs.

(c) The wages and salaries control account which acts as a control over the entries in the accounts. There are different ways of writing up this control account, but the way used by AAT is to use this account to control the gross pay and deductions from the employees, plus employers' NIC.

6.2 Double entry

The double entry reflects these two fundamentals and uses three main accounts – the wages and salaries control account, the wages expense account and the PAYE/NIC account.

1   Dr   Wages expense account
        Cr   Wages and salaries control account
    with the gross wages of the employees.

2   Dr   Wages and salaries control account
        Cr   Bank account
    with the net wages paid to the employees

3   Dr   Wages and salaries control account
        Cr   PAYE/NIC account
    with those deductions made from the employees which are payable to the HM revenue and customs

4   Dr   Wages expense account
        Cr   Wages and salaries control account
    Dr   Wages and salaries control account
        Cr   PAYE/NIC account
    with the employer's NI contributions

Example

The wages and salaries information for an organisation for a week is given as follows:

	£
Gross wages	34,000
PAYE deducted	7,400
NIC deducted	5,600
Net pay	21,000
Employer's NIC	7,800

Write up the relevant ledger accounts in the general ledger to reflect this.

Solution

Wages and salaries control account

		£			£
2	Bank account	21,000	1	Wages expense account	34,000
			4	Wages expense account (ers NIC)	7,800
3	PAYE/NIC account (PAYE)	7,400			
3	PAYE/NIC account (ees NIC)	5,600			
4	PAYE/NIC account (ers NIC)	7,800			
		41,800			41,800

Wages expense account

		£			£
1	Wages and salaries control	34,000			
4	Wages and salaries control (ers NIC)	7,800	Bal c/d		41,800
		41,800			41,800

PAYE/NIC account

	£			£
		3	Wages and salaries control	7,400
		3	Wages and salaries control	5,600
Bal c/d	20,800	4	Wages and salaries control	7,800
	20,800			20,800
		Bal b/d		20,800

6.3 Commentary on the solution

(a) The wages and salaries control account controls the total gross wages plus the employer's NIC and the amounts paid to the employees, and other organisations (e.g.HM Revenue and Customs for PAYE and NIC). The total gross pay is taken from the company payroll as are the deductions. Assuming that the company payroll schedule reconciles and no errors are made when posting the payroll totals to the account, the account should have a nil balance.

(b) The wages expense account shows the total cost to the employer of employing the workforce (£41,800). This is the gross wages cost plus the employer's own NIC cost.

(c) The PAYE/NIC account shows the amount due to be paid over to HM Revenue and Customs, i.e. PAYE, employee's NIC plus the employer's NIC.

Activity 2

Given below is a summary of an organisation's payroll details for a week. You are required to prepare the journals to enter the figures in the general ledger accounts and to state the balance on the control account, once the net amount has been paid to the employees.

	£
Gross wages	54,440
PAYE	11,840
Employee's NIC	8,960
Employer's NIC	12,480

7 Summary

This chapter has introduced the fairly complex taxation elements that affect the payment of wages and salaries. You need to understand in principle how PAYE and NI works and be able to calculate the net pay to employees given the PAYE and NI deductions. However, you do not need to be able to use HM Revenue and Customs tables. Most importantly you do need to understand how wages and salaries are accounted for in the general ledger.

Answers to chapter activities

Activity 1

B   The employer

Activity 2

1   Dr   Wages expense account
        Cr   Wages and salaries control account
with the gross wages of £54,440

2   Dr   Wages expense account
        Cr   Wages and salaries control account
with the employer's NI contributions of £12, 480

3   Dr   Wages and salaries control account
        Cr   PAYE/NIC account
with the PAYE of £11,840, and with the employee's NIC of £8,960 and with the employer's NIC of £12,480

Once the net amount to be paid to the employee has been posted by debiting the wages and salaries control account and crediting the bank account with £33,640, the balance on the control account will be nil.

8   Test your knowledge

Workbook Activity 3

An employee has gross pay for a week of £368.70. The PAYE for the week is £46.45, the employer's NIC £30.97 and the employee's NIC £23.96.

What is the employee's net pay for the week?

Workbook Activity 4

Given below is the wages book for the month of May 20X1 for a small business with four employees.

Wages book

Employee number	Gross pay	PAYE	Employee's NIC	Employer's NIC	Net pay
	£	£	£	£	£
001	1,200	151	78	101	971
002	1,400	176	91	118	1,133
003	900	113	58	76	729
004	1,550	195	101	130	1,254
	5,050	635	328	425	4,087

You are required to use the totals from the wages book for the month to write up journal entries to record:

- The wages expense

- The HM Revenue and Customs liability

- The net wages paid to the employees

You can then record these entries in the ledger accounts below.

Gross wages control account			
	£		£

Wages expense account			
	£		£
30 April	Balance b/d	23,446	

HM Revenue and Customs account				
		£		£
19 May	CPB	760	30 April	Balance b/d	760

Petty cash systems

6

Introduction

When studying Basic Accounting I we were introduced to the purpose of petty cash and how it is recorded within the petty cash book. We also saw how this data was then transferred into the general ledger.

In this chapter, we will look in more detail at further aspects of petty cash, including the techniques we can use to control and reconcile the balances.

SKILLS
1.1 Prepare petty cash vouchers
1.2 Calculate the purchase tax (e.g. VAT) where the expense includes it
2.1 List the petty cash vouchers into an analysed petty cash book ensuring that the expenses are entered and analysed
2.2 Account for any tax paid (e.g. VAT)
2.3 Total and cross cast the petty cash book
3.1 Balance off the petty cash book using the imprest system
3.2 Reconcile the petty cash book with cash in hand
3.3 Prepare a petty cash reimbursement request or equivalent
3.4 Show the reimbursement of the petty cash expenditure in the petty cash book

CONTENTS
1 Petty cash vouchers
2 Maintaining petty cash records
3 Petty cash control account
4 Reconciling the petty cash

1 Petty cash vouchers

1.1 Introduction

We have already seen in Basic Accounting I the importance of petty cash vouchers as any payment of petty cash should not be made unless supported by a properly completed petty cash voucher which has been authorised.

1.2 Completing a petty cash voucher

If an employee wishes to be reimbursed for a business expense that he has incurred himself then he must complete a petty cash voucher. Different businesses will have different policies regarding amounts that can be paid out as petty cash but most organisations will require that petty cash vouchers are supported by documentation to show that the expenditure has occurred.

Most businesses will require petty cash vouchers to be supported by a receipt or other evidence of the payment such as a train ticket for a train fare.

Example

The petty cashier for your organisation is on holiday and you have been asked to act as petty cashier in her absence. You have been given the policy documents relating to petty cash and have discovered the following:

- a petty cash system is operated with an imprest amount of £300 per week;

- no single petty cash voucher for more than £30 can be paid out of petty cash; any claims for amounts greater than £30 must be made using a cheque requisition;

- all petty cash claims other than taxi fares (see below) must include a valid receipt or evidence of payment;

- taxi fares of less than £5 can be paid without a receipt; all others must be supported by a receipt from the taxi;

- other transport expenses such as rail or underground fares exceeding £3 must be supported by a ticket showing the price of the fare or evidence of payment of the fare;

- other transport expenses of less than £3 do not need evidence of payment;

- no single employee can make claims of more than £30 on any one day.

On your first day of acting as petty cashier you have to deal with the following petty cash vouchers.

PETTY CASH VOUCHER				
Authorised by	*Received by* P Mallins	*No*		3562
Date	*Description*	*Amount*		
12 June X6	Tea and biscuits for office	12	73	
	Total	12	73	

Receipt attached

PETTY CASH VOUCHER				
Authorised by	*Received by* R Nixon	*No*		3563
Date	*Description*	*Amount*		
12 June X6	Taxi	3	80	
	Total	3	80	

PETTY CASH VOUCHER				
Authorised by	Received by J Karl		No	3564
Date	Description		Amount	
12 June X6	Bus fare		2	50
	Total		2	50

PETTY CASH VOUCHER				
Authorised by	Received by G Hull		No	3565
Date	Description		Amount	
12 June X6	Taxi		6	00
	Total		6	00

PETTY CASH VOUCHER				
Authorised by	Received by F Trent		No	3566
Date	Description		Amount	
12 June X6	Train fare		12	80
	Total		12	80

Ticket attached

PETTY CASH VOUCHER			
Authorised by	Received by P Phillips	No	3567
Date	Description	Amount	
12 June X6	Entertaining	35	00
	Total	35	00

PETTY CASH VOUCHER			
Authorised by	Received by V Close	No	3568
Date	Description	Amount	
12 June X6	Underground ticket	3	60
	Total	3	60

PETTY CASH VOUCHER			
Authorised by	Received by P Mallins	No	3569
Date	Description	Amount	
12 June X6	Entertaining	20	00
	Total	20	00

Restaurant bill attached

For each voucher explain whether you would be able to authorise it for payment from petty cash.

You must check each petty cash voucher carefully, together with any supporting documentation, to ensure that a valid payment can be made.

Solution

Voucher 3562 – Amount is less than £30 and supported by receipt – authorise for payment.

Voucher 3563 – Taxi fare of less than £5 therefore no receipt required – authorise for payment.

Voucher 3564 – Bus fare of less than £3 therefore no receipt required – authorise for payment.

Voucher 3565 – Taxi fare of more than £5 but no receipt – cannot authorise for payment.

Voucher 3566 – Train fare with ticket attached – authorise for payment.

Voucher 3567 – Claim for more than £30 – cannot authorise for payment – cheque requisition required.

Voucher 3568 – Underground ticket for more than £3 but no evidence of payment – cannot authorise for payment.

Voucher 3569 – Claim made by P Mallins who has already claimed £12.73 today (voucher no 3562) making a total of £32.73 – cannot authorise for payment.

1.3 Sales tax and petty cash vouchers

If an expense includes an amount of sales tax, then the amounts recorded on the petty cash vouchers should be the net amount, the amount of sales tax and the total payment.

Activity 1

You are the petty cashier for your organisation. During your lunch break five receipts have appeared on your desk from employees making petty cash claims.

The receipts are as follows:

£2.99	Chocolate biscuits
£6.00	Stationery (includes sales tax at 20%)
£24.00	Computer disks (includes sales tax at 20%)
£8.90	Train fare
£3.95	Coffee and milk

The last petty cash voucher to be used was number 158. You are required to fill out and authorise petty cash vouchers for each of these receipts ready for payment of the petty cash to the employees concerned. Use the blank petty cash vouchers given.

Today's date is 7 September 20X1.

PETTY CASH VOUCHER			
Authorised by	Received by		No
Date	Description		Amount
		Total	

PETTY CASH VOUCHER			
Authorised by	Received by		No
Date	Description		Amount
		Total	

PETTY CASH VOUCHER			
Authorised by	Received by	No	
Date	Description	Amount	
	Total		

PETTY CASH VOUCHER			
Authorised by	Received by	No	
Date	Description	Amount	
	Total		

PETTY CASH VOUCHER			
Authorised by	Received by	No	
Date	Description	Amount	
	Total		

KAPLAN PUBLISHING

2 Maintaining petty cash records

2.1 Introduction

Basic accounting I introduced us to the layout of the petty cash book, but it is worth recapping the format here.

2.2 Layout of the petty cash book

The petty cash book is normally set out as a large ledger account with a small receipts side and a larger analysed payments side. A typical petty cash book is set out below.

Receipts			Payments								
Date	Narrative	Total	Date	Narrative	Voucher no	Total £	Postage £	Cleaning £	Tea & Coffee £	Sundry £	Sales tax £
1 Nov	Bal b/d	35.50									
1 Nov	Cheque 394	114.50	1 Nov	ASDA	58	23.50			23.50		
			2 Nov	Post Office Ltd	59	29.50	29.50				
			2 Nov	Cleaning materials	60	15.08		12.57			2.51
			3 Nov	Postage	61	16.19	16.19				
			3 Nov	ASDA	62	10.57		8.81			1.76
			4 Nov	Newspapers	63	18.90				18.90	
			5 Nov	ASDA	64	12.10				10.09	2.01

2.3 Writing up the petty cash book

When cash is originally paid into the petty cash book then this will be recorded on the receipts side (debit side) of the petty cash book.

Each petty cash voucher will then in turn be written up in the petty cash book on the payments side, ensuring they are recorded in their pre-numbered order, and with each item of expenditure being recorded in the correct analysis column.

Example

A business has just started to run a petty cash system with an imprest amount of £100. £100 is withdrawn from the bank account and paid into the petty cash box on 3 April 20X1.

During the first week the following authorised petty cash vouchers were paid. These transactions will now be recorded in the petty cash book.

PETTY CASH VOUCHER				
Authorised by T Smedley	Received by P Lannall		No	0001
Date	Description		Amount	
3 April 20X1	Tea/coffee/milk		4	73
		Total	4	73

PETTY CASH VOUCHER				
Authorised by T Smedley	Received by R Sellers		No	0002
Date	Description		Amount	
3 April 20X1	Train fare		14	90
		Total	14	90

PETTY CASH VOUCHER				
Authorised by	Received by	No		0003
T Smedley	F Dorne			
Date	Description	Amount		
4 April 20X1	Stationery		4	00
	Sales tax		0	80
	Total		4	80

PETTY CASH VOUCHER				
Authorised by	Received by	No		0004
T Smedley	P Dent			
Date	Description	Amount		
5 April 20X1	Postage costs		16	35
	Total		16	35

PETTY CASH VOUCHER				
Authorised by	Received by	No		0005
T Smedley	H Polly			
Date	Description	Amount		
7 April 20X1	Train fare		15	30
	Total		15	30

PETTY CASH VOUCHER				
Authorised by T Smedley	*Received by* P Lannall		*No*	0006
Date	*Description*		*Amount*	
8 April 20X1	Milk/biscuits		3	85
		Total	3	85

Solution

Petty cash book

Receipts			**Payments**								
Date	Narrative	Total	Date	Narrative	Voucher no	Total	Postage	Travel	Tea & coffee	Sundry	Sales tax
20X1		£	20X1			£	£	£	£	£	£
03/04	Cash	100.00	03/04	Tea/coffee	0001	4.73			4.73		
			03/04	Train fare	0002	14.90		14.90			
			04/04	Stationery	0003	4.70				4.00	0.80
			05/04	Postage	0004	16.35	16.35				
			07/04	Train fare	0005	15.30		15.30			
			08/04	Milk/biscuits	0006	3.85			3.85		

2.4 The imprest system

Many businesses use the imprest system for petty cash. Using an imprest system makes petty cash easier to control and therefore reduces the possibility of error and fraud.

The business decides on a fixed amount of petty cash (the imprest) which is just large enough to cover normal petty cash requirements for a period (usually a week). This amount of petty cash is withdrawn from the bank.

Claims are paid out of petty cash by a voucher being completed for each amount of petty cash paid out. The vouchers are kept in the petty cash box so that the amount of cash held decreases and is replaced by vouchers.

At any given time, the total contents of the box (i.e. petty cash plus amounts withdrawn represented by vouchers) should equal the amount of the imprest.

At the end of the period, a cheque is drawn for the total of the vouchers which restores the petty cash float to the amount of the imprest. The vouchers are removed from the petty cash box and filed.

> ### ☀ Example
>
> The imprest amount for a petty cash system is £150, which is the amount paid into the petty cash box on 1 November. At the end of the week the total of the vouchers in the petty cash box is £125.05. How much cash is required in order to replenish the petty cash box to the imprest amount?
>
> **Solution**
>
> £125.05, the amount paid out on the basis of the petty cash vouchers.

> ### 📝 Activity 2
>
> Allsports Limited maintains an imprest amount for the petty cash of £250. During the current period, the sum of £180 is paid out, supported by petty cash vouchers. At the end of the period, what amount should be drawn out of the bank?

2.5 Non-imprest petty cash system

An imprest petty cash system as in the previous example is the most common method of dealing with and controlling petty cash. However some businesses may use a non-imprest system. This might be where a set amount of cash is withdrawn each week and paid into the petty cash box no matter what the level of expenditure in that week.

For example it may be an organisation's policy to cash a cheque for £50 each Monday morning for use as petty cash for the week. The danger here is either that petty cash requirements are more than £50 in the week in which case the petty cash box will run out of money. Alternatively week after week expenditure is significantly less than £50 each week, leading to a large amount of cash building up in the petty cash box.

> ### 📝 Activity 3
>
> Give two ways in which the company might attempt to maintain security over petty cash.

3 Petty cash control account

3.1 Introduction

In most cases the petty cash book is not only a book of prime entry but also part of the general ledger. However in other businesses the petty cash book will be simply a book of prime entry and a petty cash control account will be maintained in the general ledger.

3.2 Petty cash control account

The petty cash control account summarises the information in the petty cash book and is posted from the petty cash book. When cash is put into the petty cash box the petty cash control account will be debited and the total of the petty cash payments for the period will be credited to the petty cash control account.

Example

A business runs a petty cash imprest system with an imprest amount of £100. At 1 May there was £32.56 remaining in the petty cash box and £67.44 of cash was withdrawn from the bank and put into the petty cash box to restore the imprest amount. During the month of May the total payments from the petty cash book were £82.16.

Write up the petty cash control account.

Solution

Petty cash control account

	£		£
Balance b/f	32.56	Payments	82.16
Receipt from bank	67.44	Balance c/d	17.84
	_____		_____
	100.00		100.00
	_____		_____
Balance b/d	17.84		

3.3 Reconciliation of the petty cash with the petty cash control account

The balance on the petty cash control account at the end of each period should be equal to the amount of cash remaining in the petty cash box. If there is a difference then this must be investigated.

3.4 Possible causes of difference

If there is more cash in the petty cash box than the balance on the petty cash control account this could be due to an error in writing up the petty cash book as more has been recorded in payments than has actually been paid out. In this case the entries in the petty cash book should be checked to the underlying petty cash vouchers to discover the error.

If there is less cash in the petty cash box than the balance on the petty cash control account this could also be due to an error in writing up the petty cash book as this time less payments have been recorded in the petty cash control account than were actually made. This may be due to a petty cash voucher having been omitted from the petty cash book and therefore again the underlying petty cash vouchers should all be checked to their entries in the petty cash book.

If no accounting errors or posting errors can be found then the cause is likely to be one of the following:

- an error has been made in paying a petty cash voucher and more money was handed out than was recorded on the voucher;

- cash has been paid out of the petty cash box without a supporting voucher;

- cash could have been stolen from the petty cash box.

In such cases the matter should be investigated and security of the petty cash and petty cash procedures improved.

Example

The petty cash control account from the previous example is reproduced.

Petty cash control account

	£		£
Balance b/f	32.56	Payments	82.16
Receipt	67.44	Balance c/d	17.84
	100.00		100.00
Balance b/d	17.84		

What action should be taken if when the petty cash was counted at 31 May the amount held in the box was:

(a) £27.84

(b) £7.84

Solution

(a) If the amount of cash in the box was £27.84 then this is £10 more than expected. The following checks should be made:

Has the balance on the petty cash control account been correctly calculated?

- Have the receipt and payments totals been correctly posted to the petty cash control account?

- Have the payments in the petty cash book been correctly totalled?

- Has each individual petty cash voucher been correctly recorded in the petty cash book?

(b) If the amount of cash in the box is only £7.84 then this is £10 less than expected. All of the above checks should be carried out and if no accounting errors can be found then it will have to be assumed that either £10 too much has been paid out on a petty cash voucher, £10 has been paid out of the petty cash box without a supporting voucher or that £10 has been stolen from the petty cash box.

4 Reconciling the petty cash

4.1 Introduction

We saw earlier in the chapter that when an imprest system is being used for petty cash then at any point in time the amount of cash in the petty cash box plus the total of the vouchers in the petty cash box should equal the imprest amount.

At regular intervals, usually at the end of each week, this check will be carried out.

4.2 Procedure for reconciling the petty cash box

The total amount of cash in the petty cash box will be counted. The vouchers that have been paid during the week are also in the petty cash box and they must also be totalled.

When the amount of cash is added to the total of the vouchers in the box they should equal the imprest amount.

The petty cash vouchers for the week will then be removed from the box and filed.

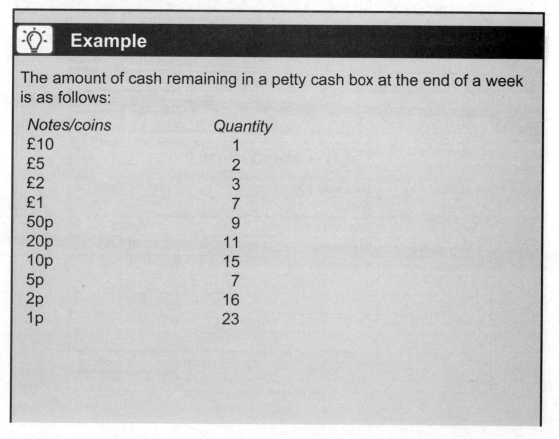

Example

The amount of cash remaining in a petty cash box at the end of a week is as follows:

Notes/coins	Quantity
£10	1
£5	2
£2	3
£1	7
50p	9
20p	11
10p	15
5p	7
2p	16
1p	23

The imprest amount is £100 and the vouchers in the petty cash box at the end of the week are as follows:

PETTY CASH VOUCHER				
Authorised by C Alexi	*Received by* P Trant		*No*	0467
Date	*Description*		*Amount*	
4 May 20X3	Window cleaner		15	00
		Total	15	00

PETTY CASH VOUCHER				
Authorised by C Alexi	*Received by* F Saint		*No*	0468
Date	*Description*		*Amount*	
5 May 20X3	Train fare		9	80
		Total	9	80

PETTY CASH VOUCHER				
Authorised by C Alexi	*Received by* A Paul		*No*	0469
Date	*Description*		*Amount*	
5 May 20X3	Stationery		8	00
	Sales tax		1	60
		Total	9	60

PETTY CASH VOUCHER				
Authorised by C Alexi	*Received by* P Peters		*No*	0470
Date	*Description*		*Amount*	
7 May 20X3	Postage		6	80
	Total		6	80

PETTY CASH VOUCHER				
Authorised by C Alexi	*Received by* C Ralph		*No*	0471
Date	*Description*		*Amount*	
5 May 20X3	Train fare		16	90
	Total		16	90

The cash and vouchers in the petty cash box at the end of the week are to be reconciled.

Solution

The petty cash must be totalled:

Notes/coins	Quantity	Amount £
£10	1	10.00
£5	2	10.00
£2	3	6.00
£1	7	7.00
50p	9	4.50
20p	11	2.20
10p	15	1.50
5p	7	0.35
2p	16	0.32
1p	23	0.23
		42.10

Now the vouchers must be totalled.

	£
0467	15.00
0468	9.80
0469	9.40
0470	6.80
0471	16.90
	57.90

Finally, total the cash and the vouchers to ensure that they add back to the imprest amount.

	£
Cash	42.10
Vouchers	57.90
	100.00

Activity 4

Your business runs a petty cash box based upon an imprest amount of £60. This morning you have emptied the petty cash box and found the following notes, coins and vouchers.

Notes
£5 × 2

Coins
£1 × 3
50p × 5
20p × 4
10p × 6
5p × 7
2p × 10
1p × 8

Vouchers	£
2143	10.56
2144	3.30
2145	9.80
2146	8.44
2147	2.62
2148	6.31
2149	1.44

You are required to reconcile the cash and the vouchers in the petty cash box.

5 Summary

In this chapter we have considered the entire petty cash system. Cash is paid into the petty cash box in order to meet the requirements for actual cash in a business's life. This will normally be in the form of reimbursing employees for business expenses that they have incurred on their own behalf. In order to be reimbursed for the expense, the employee must fill out a petty cash voucher which will normally be accompanied by a receipt for the expense and must then be authorised. At this point the employee can be paid the cash out of the petty cash box.

All petty cash is recorded in the petty cash book which is normally both a book of prime entry and part of the general ledger. The cash paid into the petty cash box is recorded as a receipt in the petty cash book and as a payment in the cash payments book, an amount of cash being taken out of the bank account. The payments of petty cash vouchers are recorded as payments in the petty cash book and are analysed as to the type of payment. These payments are then recorded as debit entries in the appropriate expense account.

At the end of a period, a week or a month possibly, the cash in the petty cash box will be counted and reconciled to the vouchers in the box. In an imprest system the total of the vouchers in the box plus the total of the cash in the box should equal the imprest amount.

Answers to chapter activities

Activity 1

PETTY CASH VOUCHER				
Authorised by A Student	Received by		No	159
Date	Description		Amount	
07/09/X1	Chocolate biscuits		2	99
	Total		2	99

PETTY CASH VOUCHER				
Authorised by A Student	Received by		No	160
Date	Description		Amount	
07/09/X1	Stationery		5	00
	Sales tax		1	00
	Total		6	00

PETTY CASH VOUCHER				
Authorised by A Student	Received by		No	161
Date	Description		Amount	
07/09/X1	Computer disks		20	00
	Sales tax		4	00
	Total		24	00

PETTY CASH VOUCHER				
Authorised by A Student	Received by		No	162
Date	Description		Amount	
07/09/X1	Train fare		8	90
	Total		8	90

PETTY CASH VOUCHER				
Authorised by A Student	Received by		No	163
Date	Description		Amount	
07/09/X1	Coffee and milk		3	95
	Total		3	95

If any petty cash expenses include sales tax then the sales tax must be shown on the petty cash voucher so that it can eventually be correctly posted to the petty cash book and expense accounts.

Activity 2

£180

Activity 3

Any two from the following:

(i)   Should be kept securely in a locked box or safe, etc.

(ii) All payments should be properly authorised.

(iii) Should be the responsibility of one person.

(iv) The amount of any one payment should be restricted.

Activity 4

Notes and coins

	£	£
£5 × 2	10.00	
£1 × 3	3.00	
50p × 5	2.50	
20p × 4	0.80	
10p × 6	0.60	
5p × 7	0.35	
2p × 10	0.20	
1p × 8	0.08	
	————	
		17.53

Vouchers

2143	10.56	
2144	3.30	
2145	9.80	
2146	8.44	
2147	2.62	
2148	6.31	
2149	1.44	
	————	
		42.47
		————
Imprest amount		60.00
		————

6 Test your knowledge

Workbook Activity 5

Given below are the petty cash vouchers that have been paid during the week ending 12 January 20X1 out of a petty cash box run on an imprest system of £150 per week. At the end of each week a cheque requisition is drawn up for a cheque for cash to bring the petty cash box back to the imprest amount.

Voucher no	Amount £	Reason
03526	13.68	Postage
03527	25.00	Staff welfare
03528	15.12	Stationery (including £2.52 sales tax)
03529	12.00	Taxi fare (including £2.00 sales tax)
03530	6.40	Staff welfare
03531	12.57	Postage
03532	6.80	Rail fare
03533	9.60	Stationery (including £1.60 sales tax)
03534	19.20	Taxi fare (including £3.20 sales tax)

You are required to:

- write up the petty cash book given;

- prepare the cheque requisition for the cash required to restore the petty cash box to the imprest amount;

- post the petty cash book totals to the general ledger accounts given.

Petty cash book

Receipts			Payments								
Date	Narrative	Total	Date	Narrative	Voucher no	Total £	Postage £	Staff welfare £	Station-ery £	Travel expenses £	Sales tax £

CHEQUE REQUISITION FORM

CHEQUE DETAILS

Date ....

Payee ....

Amount £ ....

Reason .... Account code........................

Invoice no. (attached/to follow) ....

Receipt (attached/to follow)................... ....

Required by (Print)............................... ....

Signature...

Authorised by: ....

General ledger accounts

Postage account

		£			£
5 Jan	Balance b/d	248.68			

Staff welfare account

		£			£
5 Jan	Balance b/d	225.47			

Stationery account

	£		£
5 Jan Balance b/d	176.57		

Travel expenses account

	£		£
5 Jan Balance b/d	160.90		

Postage account

	£		£
		5 Jan Balance b/d	2,385.78

Workbook Activity 6

A business runs its petty cash on an imprest system with an imprest amount of £100 per week.

At the end of the week ending 22 May 20X1 the vouchers in the petty cash box were:

Voucher no	£
02634	13.73
02635	8.91
02636	10.57
02637	3.21
02638	11.30
02639	14.66

The cash remaining in the petty cash box was made up as follows:

£10 note	1
£5 note	2
£2 coin	3
£1 coin	7
50p coin	5
20p coin	4
10p coin	1
5p coin	2
2p coin	3
1p coin	6

You are required to reconcile the petty cash in the box to the vouchers in the box at 22 May 20X1 and if it does not reconcile to suggest reasons for the difference.

7

The banking system

Introduction

This chapter will introduce you to the banking system and the terminology used within this system.

SKILLS	CONTENTS
1.1 Identify the main services offered by banks and building societies	**1** Bank and customer relationship
1.2 Describe how the banking clearing system works	**2** Banking services
	3 Banking procedures
1.3 Identify different forms of payment which include	**4** The clearing system
	5 Cheques
– cash	**6** Cheque crossings
– cheques	**7** Transferring money by different methods
– credit cards	**8** Credit cards and debit cards
– debit cards	**9** Banking documentation
– direct payments	
1.4 Identify the information required to ensure the following payments are valid	
– cash	
– cheques	
– credit cards	
– debit cards	
1.5 Describe the processing security procedures relating to the different forms of payment	

1 Bank and customer relationship

1.1 Introduction

The relationship between the bank and the customer can be described best as that of a receivable and payable.

1.2 Receivable/payable relationship

This is the basic bank/customer relationship. If the bank holds money belonging to the customer, the money has to be repaid at some time, and therefore from the bank's point of view, the customer is the **payable** (i.e. the bank owes money). From the customer's point of view the bank is the receivable (i.e. the customer is owed money by the bank).

However, when the customer borrows money from the bank the relationship is reversed. For the bank the customer is the **receivable** and for the customer the bank is the **payable**.

This is the case not only if a business has a loan from the bank but also if the business has an overdraft with a bank. In this situation the business owes the bank money.

1.3 Banking terminology

The usual meanings of debit and credit in double entry bookkeeping in the context of cash are:

*   debit – money into the bank account;
*   credit – money out of the bank account.

On a bank statement these meanings are reversed as the statement is prepared from the bank's point of view, that is:

Debit
or
Increase in a receivable (e.g. increase in overdraft)
Decrease in a payable (e.g. decrease in cash balance)

Credit
or
Decrease in a receivable (e.g. decrease in overdraft)
Increase in payable (e.g. increase in cash balance)

When a customer has money in the bank account this is described by the bank as a credit balance. If the customer has an overdraft then this is described as a debit balance.

1.4 Customer's duties

The law states that if the bank holds the customer's money, it is up to the customer to ask for the money back. This is unusual, because normally the onus is on the person who owes the money to repay it.

The customer must be careful when writing cheques so as not to mislead the bank or make forgery easy.

The customer's request for repayment must be in writing (e.g. a cheque).

1.5 Legal relationship between banker and customer

In law there is technically a contract between the banker and his customer. This means that not only does the customer have duties to perform but also the bank has certain rights and duties within the relationship.

The duties of the bank include:

- paying a customer's cheques when there are sufficient funds in the account;
- keeping the details of a customer's account secret;
- sending bank statements to customers;
- to follow the customer's instructions for payment such as a standing order (see later in the chapter);
- to accept cash and cheques paid in by the customer and to credit the customer's account;
- to exercise proper skill and care.

The legal nature of the relationship means that if the bank fails in these duties and the customer suffers losses then the customer could sue the bank. For example if a bank failed to pay a properly completed cheque to a supplier and that supplier cuts off supplies, the bank's customer who wrote the cheque could sue the bank for any losses suffered.

2 Banking services

2.1 Introduction

Traditionally, there was more of a difference between the services offered by banks and those offered by building societies. However since banking laws were changed, building societies are able to offer more services that are equivalent to those offered by banks. People and businesses have bank accounts so they do not have to keep all their money as cash.

There are three main types of bank account:

- current accounts;
- deposit or savings accounts;
- loan accounts.

2.2   Current accounts

The current account is a business's normal working account. Cash and cheques received from customers are paid into this account and the business will be issued with a cheque book so that expenses and suppliers can be paid by writing cheques.

Current accounts are also the most common form of account for personal customers. A personal customer will normally be issued with a cheque book, a cheque guarantee card (see later in the chapter) and a card for use in the automated cash machines.

Many current accounts now pay a low rate of interest on any credit balances.

2.3   Overdraft

Most banks, on request, will allow a business (or indeed a personal customer) an agreed level of overdraft. This means that on occasions if the current account does not have enough funds to cover cheques written the bank will still honour those cheques up to the overdraft limit. The bank will charge interest on any overdrawn balances and often an arrangement fee for the setting up of the overdraft facility.

2.4   Deposit accounts

Deposit accounts, or savings accounts, are held by many business and personal customers. A business can use a deposit account to house short-term surplus funds as the interest earned on deposit account balances is often considerably higher than that on current account balances. Money in deposit accounts can then be transferred to the current account when required but some types of account do require a period of notice before funds can be transferred or removed from the account.

2.5 Loan accounts

Although an overdraft on a current account can be a useful method of short term borrowing in order to fund the everyday expenses of a business, if larger funds are required for example for the purchase of plant and machinery in a business, then a separate loan should be taken out.

A business loan can be made to all types of business and will normally be secured. This means that the bank will have rights over assets of the business if the loan is not repaid or alternatively the personal guarantee of the owner of the business will be required.

For the purchase of property a commercial mortgage can be provided. This is normally for a period of 25 years and is secured on the property itself. Therefore if the mortgage is not repaid, the bank can sell the property in order to get its money back.

3 Banking procedures

3.1 Getting payment for the customer

When a customer pays a cheque into their bank account which has been received from another person, the customer is asking the branch to obtain payment from the other person's bank account and credit it to (i.e. pay it into) his or her bank account.

The bank has a duty to:

- credit the customer's account with the value of the cheques presented by the customer;
- collect the money from the third party;
- credit the money to the correct account.

3.2 Paying in cash and cheques

The individual who is paying in monies takes the cash, cheques and paying in book to the bank and hands them to the cashier behind the counter.

The cashier:

- agrees the items to be paid in against the information on the paying-in slip (this is typically a two part document which comes bound in a book holding about 20 or 30 such documents; one part of the document is a 'stub' which is retained by the customer, the other part is retained by the bank);

- checks the other details on the paying-in slip (e.g. date, payee);

- stamps both parts of the slip;

- removes the bank's copy, leaving the paying-in stub as the customer's record;

- returns the paying-in book.

Any cash paid in will be credited direct to the business's account when the branch records all the transactions for the day.

Cheques paid in are sorted and put through the clearing system.

4 The clearing system

4.1 Introduction

The major banks have developed a system known as the clearing system which is the method by which the banks exchange cheques.

Most of the UK high street banks are involved in this system.

4.2 How the clearing system works

The whole process of clearing cheques takes three working days.

Day 1

The branch of the bank (the collecting bank) will have received cheques paid in by customers written by third parties who have their accounts at:

- other clearing banks;

- other branches of the same bank.

At the end of the day these cheques are:

- sorted by the bank;

- stamped with details of the branch/bank;

- processed through a machine which puts the amount payable onto the bottom of the cheque in code.

The cheques are then sent by courier to the bank's own clearing department.

Day 2

The bank's clearing department receives cheques from all its branches. It will now:

- sort the cheques by bank;

- take other banks' cheques to the Central Clearing House;

- send the cheques relating to its own branches to those branches without sending them to the clearing house (this is inter-branch clearing).

The central clearing house arranges for all the banks involved to attend to 'swap' cheques and to arrange for any differences in the values of cheques swapped to be paid on the following day.

The clearing departments of the banks then receive the cheques which have been written by their customers. The clearing department of each bank will:

- sort the cheques by branch using a machine which reads the code on each cheque;

- record the cheque information into the bank computer (to debit customers' accounts by the amounts paid on the cheques);

- send the paid cheques to the paying customers' branches.

Day 3

Each branch receives the cheques written by its own customers. The branch has to check that the cheque is valid and to return any cheques that cannot be paid.

Any cheques which cannot be paid are sent by first class post to the branch that collected them (shown by the stamp placed on the cheque on day 1).

4.3   Clearing debts

The clearing process results in banks owing money to each other.

Each clearing bank maintains an account with the Bank of England. These accounts are known as **operational balances**. These balances are used to settle the debts which arise between the banks in the course of clearing.

Cheques which are written by an account holder at the same branch do not leave the branch.

Cheques which are written by an account holder of a different branch of the same bank go from the bank's own clearing department to the other branch.

The operation of the clearing system means that when cheques are paid into a bank account it will take three working days before they are credited to the organisation's bank account.

> ### ✍ Activity 1
>
> David Cater has received a cheque for £1,000 from MEL Motor Factors Limited and has paid it into his account at the Mid-West Bank. When he asks if he can draw out some cash against the cheque, he is told by the cashier that he will have to wait four days from the date that the cheque was paid in.
>
> Explain briefly why the bank might ask David to wait before he can draw out some or all of the £1,000.

5 Cheques

> ### 🔍 Definition
>
> **Cheque** – An unconditional order in writing signed by the drawer, requiring a bank to pay on demand a sum certain in money to a named person or to the bearer.

5.1 Detailed meaning of the definition

1	**Unconditional**	Payment cannot depend upon the outcome of events, e.g. 'pay Mr Brown £75 provided my salary cheque has been paid into my account'.
2	**Writing**	A cheque must be in writing. Pen, biro, print or pencil can be used. Details in pencil can, however, be changed easily, and should be avoided. Most banks insist their pre-printed cheques be completed in ink.

3	**Signed**	A cheque must be signed by the drawer, that is the person wanting to pay the money who draws up the cheque.
4	**On demand**	It is expected that the cheque will be paid as soon as it is presented to the bank.
5	**A sum certain**	The amount must be definite, in both words and figures.
6	**Named person or bearer**	The cheque must be payable to a named person or to the bearer, i.e. whoever has the cheque in his or her possession. A cheque made out to 'cash' will be treated as payable to bearer.

5.2   Parties to a cheque

The parties involved in a cheque are:

- the drawer – the person writing the cheque.

- the payee – the person the cheque is to be paid to.

- the drawee – the bank upon whom the cheque is drawn, i.e. the bank who has issued the cheque book.

NATIONAL BANK PLC
18 Coventry Road
Birmingham ◄—— *The Drawee*
B13 2TU

19 – 14 – 60

2/3 ____ 20 X1

The Payee

Pay   J T Tunstill   or order

One Hundred Pounds only   £100.00

Account Payee

P DUNSTER

P. Dunster *The Drawer*

200550   19-40-60   5071247

Activity 2

The cheque shown below has been issued by Chang Fashions Limited. Give the name of:

(a)   the drawer;

(b)   the drawee;

(c)   the payee.

ROYAL BANK PLC
61 Euston Road
London
W12 6TH

19 – 14 – 60

25/5   20 X1

Pay   K Mitchell   or order

One Hundred and Fifty Pounds only   £150.00

Chang Fashions Limited

Mary Chang

200550   19-40-60   5071247

5.3   Checking cheques – the collecting bank

When the bank accepts a cheque which has been paid in by a customer, the bank must carefully review that cheque. Each item that the bank will check will be considered in turn.

5.4   Out of date cheque

A cheque can become out of date as it is only valid for six months from the date of issue. For example, a cheque dated 1 August 20X0 would be out of date if not paid into a bank account until 8 February 20X1.

5.5   Post-dated cheque

A cheque which is dated later than the day on which it is written cannot be paid in until that later date.

For example, a cheque written on 5 May 20X1 but dated 10 May 20X1 could not be paid into a bank account before 10 May 20X1.

5.6   Undated cheque

If a cheque is presented to the payee undated the payee can insert a date. The bank's cashier would normally ask the payee to do this.

If any undated cheques are accidentally accepted by the bank, the bank's date stamp can be used to insert it.

Once a date is entered on a cheque it cannot, however, be altered by the payee.

5.7   Payee's name

The payee's name should be the same as the one shown on the account that the cheque is being paid into.

If the name is different, then an endorsement is required (see below). If a cheque is presented with no payee's name then it cannot be accepted by the bank's cashier.

5.8   Words and figures

Both words and figures should be completed and should agree.

If they disagree the cheque should be returned by the bank to the drawer for amendment or for a new cheque to be issued.

A returned cheque will often be marked R/D or 'Return to drawer'.

5.9   Signature

The cheque must be signed by the drawer.

5.10   Crossings

If the cheque has a crossing (two parallel lines on the face of the cheque), it must be paid into a bank account. It cannot be exchanged for cash over the counter. Pre-printed cheques carry crossings (see later in the chapter).

The bank must carry out these checks when cheques are paid into a bank account. Therefore it is important that these details are checked by the appropriate person in the organisation before the cheques are paid in to the bank.

5.11   Stopped cheques

A customer has the right to stop a cheque right up until the banker pays it. The customer must write to the bank and give clear details of the payee's name, the cheque's number and the amount payable.

5.12 The sort code

The sort code is 6 numbers, normally presented in three pairs, e.g. 19-40-60.

This is a number that is unique to each branch of every bank. It is printed on every cheque that the particular branch issues and can be read by a computer.

Its purpose is the enable the computer to recognise the branch on which the cheque is drawn (the drawee) so that the clearing process can allocate that cheque to the correct branch.

 **Activity 3**

A cheque for £374 has been accepted by one of the cashiers in payment for a washing machine. As you record the cheque, you notice that it has been dated 1 June 20X2. Today's date is 1 June 20X3.

(a) Will payment of the cheque by the drawer's bank be affected by the incorrect date?

(b) Having noticed the error, is it acceptable for you to alter the cheque to the correct date?

6 Cheque crossings

6.1 Introduction

Given below is a typical example of a pre-printed cheque issued by a bank.

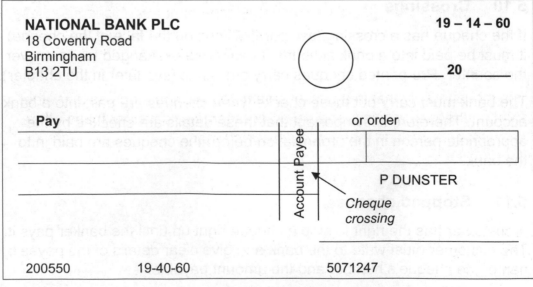

The words in the crossing will normally be in the short form 'A/c payee'.

You will see that the cheque names:

(a) the drawee: the bank paying the cheque, National Bank plc;

(b) the drawer of the cheque: the account holder who is making the payment, P Dunster.

You will also see that the cheque has two vertical parallel lines with the words 'Account payee' printed in between them. This is known as an account payee or A/c payee crossing.

🔍 Definition

A cheque crossing is an instruction to the bank, the drawee, as to how to pay the cheque.

6.2 Account payee crossing

The account payee crossing means that this cheque can only be paid into the bank account of the person named on the cheque as the payee.

Legally this crossing must now always be printed on cheques therefore this is the type of cheque crossing that you are likely to come across in practice.

6.3 Cheque endorsements

In the past, before all cheques were crossed with the words 'A/c payee' it was possible to endorse a cheque by the payee signing the reverse of the cheque with an instruction to pay a different person. Such a cheque could then be paid into the bank account of that different person.

In practice we have already seen that all pre-printed bank cheques have an account payee crossing. As this means that the cheque can only be paid into the payee's bank account then these cheques cannot be endorsed.

It is most unlikely that in an assessment you will come across any other form of cheque crossing, and we do not therefore consider these other possible crossings or their endorsements further.

7 Transferring money by different methods

7.1 Introduction

A bank customer can transfer money from his account to another person's account by two other methods which do not involve the cheque clearing system or writing cheques. These are:

* standing orders;
* direct debits.

7.2 Standing order

This is an instruction to a customer's bank to make regular payments (usually fixed amounts).

To arrange a standing order all the customer needs to do is sign a **standing order mandate** which authorises the bank to make the payments.

Standing orders are ideal for paying regular monthly bills such as insurance premiums. They can also be used to transfer money between a customer's own different accounts, e.g. transferring surplus money each month from a current account into a deposit account where it will earn interest.

7.3 Standing order mandate

To FINANCIAL BANK PLC fb

	Branch	STANDING ORDER MANDATE	

	Bank	Branch title (not address)	Sort code number
Please pay			
	Beneficiary's name		Account number
Credit			
	Amount in figures	Amount in words	
the sum of	£		
commencing	Date of first payment		Due date & frequency
	now/*	And thereafter every	
	Date and amount of last payment		
until		£	*until you receive further notice from me/us in writing
quoting the reference			and debit my/our account accordingly

Please cancel any previous standing order or direct debit in favour of the named beneficiary above

Special instructions

Account to be debited	Account number

Signature (s)

Date

_____

* Delete if not applicable

7.4 Direct debit

This is an instruction to a customer's bank to allow a third party to debit (i.e. collect money from) the customer's account at regular intervals.

Direct debits are better than standing orders when either:

- the amount is uncertain; or
- the date of payment is uncertain.

Direct debits are useful for paying items such as membership subscriptions which increase from year to year or monthly bills which alter in amount each month such as credit card bills.

Both direct debits and standing orders continue to be valid until the customer cancels or changes them.

Activity 4

Music World Limited needs to make regular monthly payments to Firmcare Finance Limited. The amount of the payment varies from month to month. Which service provided by the banks would appear to be the most appropriate?

7.5 Bank giro credit

An alternative method of transferring money into someone else's bank account is to use a bank giro credit (or credit transfer).

A bank giro credit is a method of transferring money into someone else's bank account in any bank in the country.

The system is commonly used to pay bills such as electricity, gas, credit cards, telephone.

Many businesses issue the credit transfer slip as part of their bill, or in a book. These payments are then cleared through a clearing system which is similar to the cheque clearing system.

7.6 Electronic clearing

To try to reduce the number of pieces of paper used to clear payments using the cheque clearing and giro clearing systems, a further service was introduced in 1968.

This service is known as BACS (Bankers Automated Clearing System) and is part of the clearing system.

BACS – A method of clearing payments in which transactions are recorded on magnetic tape or disks (rather than on paper). Transactions are then processed at the BACS computer centre instead of through the clearing house.

BACS can be used by banks or by companies which have been allowed to do so by the banks.

7.7 Use of BACS

BACS is used for:

* standing order payments;
* direct debits;
* salary payments;
* bank giro credits.

7.8 Telegraphic transfer

Telegraphic transfer or mail transfer may be used for large transactions that need to be processed quickly. These are electronic funds transfers between bank accounts and can be made to foreign bank accounts as well as to accounts within the UK.

To arrange an electronic funds transfer, a business must write to its bank requesting that the payment be made and enclosing details of the bank account to which the payment must be made.

7.9 CHAPS

A further service is also available to customers wishing to transfer large sums of money. This is CHAPS (Clearing House Automated Payments System).

Payments are credited to the payee on the same day as instructions are received.

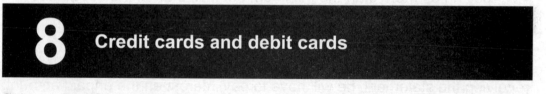

8 Credit cards and debit cards

8.1 Credit cards

Credit cards are issued by the credit card companies to allow customers to make purchases (without using cash or cheques) at certain shops, hotels, websites, etc.

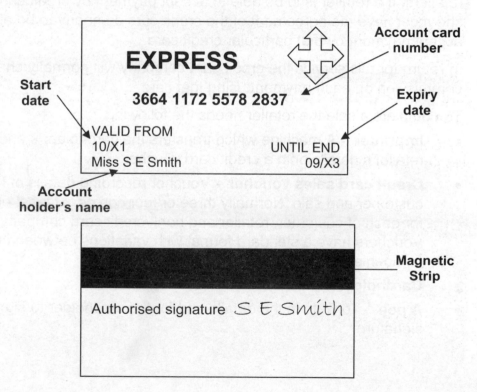

An individual opens an account with one of the credit card companies, filling in and posting off an application form. If accepted, the individual will receive a credit card.

This credit card can then be used in places which accept that particular card (they normally display a sign). The payment is recorded on a credit card sales voucher.

8.2 Payment of the credit card balance

Once a month, the credit cardholder receives a statement detailing how much he has 'spent' which is the amount he owes the credit card company.

The cardholder has a choice of:

- paying a minimum balance (set by the credit card company dependent upon the amount owed);

- paying off more than the minimum but less than the total balance outstanding;

- paying off the total balance outstanding.

If the cardholder does not pay off the total balance within 25 days of receiving the statement, he will have to pay interest on the unpaid amount.

8.3 Accepting credit cards

Businesses which make direct sales to the public are generally known as retailers. If a retailer is to be able to accept payment by credit cards, he or she must have the agreement of the credit card company to be allowed to accept payment by that particular credit card.

In return for this service the credit card company will normally charge a commission on each payment using that card.

To complete a sale the retailer needs the following.

- **Imprinter** – A machine which transfers the cardholder's and the retailer's details onto a credit card voucher.

- **Credit card sales voucher** – Voucher recording details of retailer, customer and sale. Normally three or four copies. At least one copy for each of customer, retailer and bank/credit card company. Vouchers have a standard format with variations between credit card companies.

- **Cardholder's card**.

- **A pen** – To write in the details and for the cardholder to sign their signature.

KAPLAN PUBLISHING

```
3664 1172 4478 2837          EXPRESS          10/X1  09/X3
Miss S.E. Smith      DAY      MONTH     YEAR    DEPT  SALES NO  INITIALS
   048 9133
   CHESTERS          0    8   0    8   X    2   020    115       ANO
   BOLTON
                     DESCRIPTION                    AMOUNT

 Cardholders
 signature

  S.E. Smith
                                        Books       26        95
 Cardholder's                        Book token     10        00
 Declaration: I
 promise to pay the
 total amount
 shown as payable     AUTHORISATION CODE          TOTAL  POUNDS PENCE
 together with any
 charges thereon                                          3  6  :  9  5
 subject in the
 rules of issue.      SALES VOUCHER
                      Please keep this copy for your records
```

8.4 Electronic acceptance of credit cards

Many retail organisations no longer use the mechanical imprinter in order to accept credit card payments. Instead they are electronically connected to the credit card companies and the credit card is swiped through a machine which then sends the details of the card and the payment to the credit card company. The payment is automatically authorised by the credit card company and at the end of the day the funds are automatically paid into the organisation's bank account. The use of PIN numbers for credit card payments has been introduced. Here the customer is asked to key in their PIN number to the credit card machine and, if it is correct, then the payment is accepted by the credit card company.

8.5 Debit cards

In recent years the popularity of debit cards has increased dramatically. They are a plastic card which looks very similar to a credit card but unlike a credit card no credit is given to the cardholder.

A debit card is a method of making payment direct from a bank account without having to write out a cheque. Debit cards are issued by the main banks.

When a debit card is used to make a payment the cardholder's bank account is automatically debited with the amount of the payment. The payment then appears on the customer's bank statement along with cheque payments, standing orders and direct debits.

9 Banking documentation

9.1 Bank statement

A bank statement is a statement showing how money has gone into or left a bank account, and the amount of money held in that account at a certain date. There is a standard format with a few variations between banks.

FINANCIAL BANK plc   **fb**   CONFIDENTIAL

YOU CAN BANK ON US

10 Yorkshire Street	Account CURRENT	Sheet no. 103
Headingley	MISS ELIZABETH DERBY	
Leeds LS1 1QT		
Telephone: 0113 633061		

Name and address of bank   *Name of account holder*

Statement date 31 July 20X5   Account Number 34786695

Date	Details		Withdrawals (£)	Deposits (£)	Balance (£)
28 June	Balance from sheet no. **102**				2,670.91
1 July	000354		7.95		
	Security Insurance	DD	10.15		
	Leeds Brigate	AC	50.00		
	NWWA	DD	13.03		2,589.78
2 July	Supersaver	CP	12.63		2,577.15
5 July	000349		40.00		2,537.15
8 July	000348		18.80		2,518.35
11 July	Sure Building Society	DD	327.74		
	000346		29.80		
	Deposit account	TR	250.00		1,910.81
14 July	English Gas	SO	12.50		1,898.31
17 July	000355		30.95		1,867.36
20 July	English Electricity	SO	5.00		1,862.36
22 July	000356		50.00		1,812.36
25 July	000351		11.29		1,801.07
29 July	000352		5.29		
	000350		50.00		
	PAYROLL			340.99	2,086.77
30 July	000358		26.51		
	Balance to Sheet no. **104**				2,060.26

SO	Standing order	DD	Direct debit	CP	Card purchase
AC	Automated cash	OD	Overdrawn	TR	Transfer

Closing balance

9.2 Paying money into the bank

Money may be paid into the bank account free of charge in any branch of that particular bank. Other banks may charge a small fee.

The money paid in can be:

- cash;
- cheques;
- postal orders.

The amounts to be paid in must be summarised on a paying-in slip.

9.3 Paying-in slip

A paying-in slip is a summary of details of money paid into a bank account. There is a standard format with a few variations between banks.

To be retained by receiving bank   *A/c Number where money is being paid in*

Name of account money being paid into
For the credit of TRADING COMPANY LIMITED   Account No: 50756654

Cheques, etc for collection to be included in total credit of £295.69 paid in 15/9/20X3

Details of cheques being paid in	£	brought forward	£	brought forward	£
SJ Smith	59.26				
RS Hayes	73.80				
S Bates	15.73				
Carried forward	£148.79	carried forward	£	Total cheques etc	£

Date 15/9/X3 ◄— *Date money is being paid in*

Cashier's stamp and initials

56 – 28 – 48

FINANCIAL BANK PLC

EXETER HIGH STREET

Name of person paying money in

Credit Trading Company Limited

Paid in by J Vorlott

Address/Ref No. _____

Fee	No Chqs 3

Number of cheques being paid in

£50 Notes	100	00
20 Notes	40	00
£10 Notes		
£5 Notes		
£1 and £2		
Coins	5	00
50p	1	00
20p		
Silver		90
Bronze		
Total Cash	146	90
Cheques	148	79
POs, etc.		
Total £	295	69

Details of cash being paid in

Total of cash paid in

Total of cheques paid

Paying in slip total

10 Summary

In this chapter you have been introduced to some of the details of the UK banking system. In particular you need to be aware of how the clearing system works, of the different methods of payment through the banking system and how credit and debit cards work. Of particular importance are the details regarding cheques, as you will need to understand what makes a valid cheque and be able to deal with a cheque that you receive that is not valid.

Answers to chapter activities

Activity 1

The cheque must pass through the clearing system before the Mid-West Bank knows whether or not it has been paid. In the meantime, the bank may be reluctant to allow David to draw out cash against uncleared funds.

Activity 2

(a)   Mary Chang, on behalf of Chang Fashions Limited

(b)   Royal Bank plc

(c)   K Mitchell

Activity 3

(a)   Yes. The cheque is out of date and must be re-issued by the drawer.

(b)   No.

Activity 4

Direct debit. Standing order is not appropriate since the amount of the payment varies from month to month.

11 Test your knowledge

Workbook Activity 5

Simon Harris is a self-employed accountant who has a number of clients who all pay by cheque. Today's date is 5 May 20X1 and in the last week he has received the following cheques.

Required:

Inspect each one carefully to ensure that it is valid and make a note of any problems that you find.

NATIONAL BANK PLC
18 Coventry Road
Birmingham
B13 2TU

19 – 14 – 60

30 April **20** X1

Pay S Harris   or order

One hundred and three pounds   £103.80

and 80 pence-------------------------------------   **P DUNSTER**

Account Payee

P. Dunster

LLOYD CONSTRUCTION

200550   19-14-60   5071247

WESTERN BANK PLC
21 High Street
Bristol
BS1 4TZ

20 – 15 – 60

28 April **20** X1

Pay Simon Harris   or order

Fifty pounds only --------------------------------   £50.00

Account Payee   **J Kline**

J Kline

401061   20–15–60   43215287

NORTHERN BANK PLC
68 Main Road
Warwick
B15 2KP

21– 18– 40

15 April 20 X1

Pay S Harris

or order

Forty eight pounds

£48.20

and 20 pence-------------------------------------

K T LOPEZ

Account Payee

461002   21–18–40   39761114

CENTRAL BANK PLC
44 Warwick Road
Birmingham
B6 4LK

16 – 20 – 30

1 May 20 X1

Pay S Harris

or order

One hundred and eighteen pounds

£118.50

and 50 pence-------------------------------------

A RANKIN

A Rankin

Account Payee

610400   16–20–30   32146921

NATIONAL BANK PLC
18 Coventry Road
Birmingham
B13 2TU

19 – 14 – 60

12 May 20 X1

Pay S Harris

or order

Two hundred and one pounds

£201.67

and 67 pence-------------------------------------

L GARRY

L Garry

Account Payee

201660   19-14-60   43012004

CENTRAL BANK PLC
44 Warwick Road
Birmingham
B6 4LK

16 – 20 – 30

1 May **20** X1

Pay S Harper

or order

Sixty two pounds

Account Payee

£62.50

and 50 pence-----------------------------------

L BARRETT

L Barrett

100417   16–20–30   321426107

NATIONAL BANK PLC
18 Coventry Road
Birmingham
B13 2TU

19 – 14 – 60

12 April **20** X1

Pay S Harris

or order

Forty eight pounds

Account Payee

£48.60

and 60 pence------------------------------------

F DELAWARE

F Delaware

389152   19-40-60   61298432

FIRST NATIONAL BANK PLC
Trent Park
Leeds
LS4 6OL

23 – 16 – 40

21 Oct **20** X0

Pay S Harris

or order

One hundred and thirty-seven pounds

Account Payee

£137.40

and 40 pence--------------------------------------

P IBBOTT

P Ibbott

001071   23-16-40   71294684

NATIONAL BANK PLC
18 Coventry Road
Birmingham
B13 2TU

19 – 14 – 60

28 April **20** X1

Pay S Harris

or order

One hundred and thirty five pounds

Account Payee

£153.80

and 80 pence-------------------------------------

J LOVELL

J Lovell

041261   19-14-60   32114687

CENTRAL BANK PLC
44 Warwick Road
Birmingham
B6 4LK

16 – 20 – 30

1 May **20** X1

Pay S Harris

or order

Eighty pounds

Account Payee

£80.60

and 60 pence-------------------------------------

G L ELLIS

G L eLLIS

104010   16–20–30   40162174

Workbook Activity 6

Which of the following things can NOT be determined from a customer's credit card (you can choose more than one answer).

	✓
The customer's name	
The customer's address	
The customer's credit card number	
The customer's credit limit	
The customer's credit card company	
The available amount the customer has to spend	

Workbook Activity 7

Indicate whether each of the following statements is true or false.

	True/False
When a cheque is banked the funds are available immediately	
A bank cheque has to be passed to the bank of the issue before the money becomes available	
The clearing process is quicker for a building society than for a bank	
Cheques can only be processed by banks, not building societies	
Dishonoured cheques are returned to the drawer	
The drawer has the right to stop a cheque right up until the banker pays it	

Bank reconciliations

8

Introduction

Completion of this chapter will ensure we are able to correctly prepare the cash book, compare the entries in the cash book to details on the bank statement and then finally to prepare a bank reconciliation statement.

KNOWLEDGE	
3.1	Check individual items on the bank statement accurately against the cash book to identify differences
3.2	Update the cash book from the bank statement, direct debit and standing order schedules
3.3	Prepare a bank reconciliation statement

CONTENTS	
1	Writing up the cash book
2	Preparing the bank reconciliation statement
3	Returned cheques

1 Writing up the cash book

1.1 Introduction

We were introduced to the cash book within Basic Accounting I and will review over it now for Basic Accounting II.

Most businesses will have a separate cash receipts book and a cash payments book which form part of the double entry system. If this form of record is used, the cash balance must be calculated from the opening balance at the beginning of the period, plus the receipts shown in the cash receipts book for the period and minus the payments shown in the cash payments book for the period.

1.2 Balancing the cash book

The following brief calculation will enable us to find the balance on the cash book when separate receipts and payments book are maintained.

	£
Opening balance per the cash book	X
Add: Receipts in the period	X
Less: Payments in the period	(X)
Closing balance per the cash book	X

Example

Suppose that the opening balance on the cash book is £358.72 on 1 June. During June the Cash Payments Book shows that there were total payments made of £7,326.04 during the month of June and the Cash Receipts Book shows receipts for the month of £8,132.76.

What is the closing balance on the cash book at the end of June?

Solution

		£
Opening balance at 1 June		358.72
Add:	Receipts for June	8,132.76
Less:	Payments for June	(7,326.04)
Balance at 30 June		1,165.44

Take care if the opening balance on the cash book is an overdraft balance. Any receipts in the period will reduce the overdraft and any payments will increase the overdraft.

Suppose that the opening balance on the cash book is £631.25 overdrawn on 1 June. During June the Cash Payments Book shows that there were total payments made of £2,345.42 during the month of June and the Cash Receipts Book shows receipts for the month of £1,276.45

What is the closing balance on the cash book at the end of June?

Solution

		£
Opening balance at 1 June		(631.25)
Add:	Receipts for June	1,276.45
Less:	Payments for June	(2,345.42)
Balance at 30 June		(1,700.22)

Activity 1

The opening balance at 1 January in a business cash book was £673.42 overdrawn. During January payments totalled £6,419.37 and receipts totalled £6,488.20.

What is the closing balance on the cash book?

Example

The following transactions are to be written up in the cash book of Jupiter Limited and the balance at the end of the week calculated. The opening balance on the bank account on 28 June 20X1 was £560.61.

2 July   Received a cheque for £45.90 from Hill and French Limited (no settlement discount allowed) – paying in slip 40012.

2 July   Corrected a salary error by paying a cheque for £56.89 – cheque number 100107.

3 July   Paid £96.65 by cheque to Preston Brothers after deducting a settlement discount of £1.65 – cheque number 100108.

3 July   Banked £30 of cash held – paying in slip 40013.

4 July   Received a cheque from Green and Holland for £245.89. They were allowed a settlement discount of £3.68 – paying in slip 40014.

5 July   Reimbursed the petty cash account with £34.89 of cash drawn on cheque number 100109.

The cash receipts and payments books are to be written up and the closing balance calculated.

Solution

Step 1   Enter all of the transactions into the receipts and payments cash books.

Step 2   Total the cash book columns.

Cash receipts book

Date	Narrative	Total	Sales tax	SLCA	Other	Discount
		£	£	£	£	£
20X1						
2 July	Hill and French 40012	45.90		45.90		
3 July	Cash 40013	30.00			30.00	
4 July	Green and Holland 40014	245.89		245.89		3.68
		321.79	–	291.79	30.00	3.68

Cash payments book

Date	Details	Cheque	Code no	Total	Sales tax	PLCA	Cash purchases	Other	Discounts received
				£	£	£	£	£	£
20X1									
2 July	Salary error	100107		56.89				56.89	
3 July	Preston Bros	100108		96.65		96.65			1.65
5 July	Petty cash	100109		34.89				34.89	
				188.43	–	96.65	–	91.78	1.65

Step 3 Find the balance on the cash book at the end of the week.

	£
Opening balance at 1 July	560.61
Add: Receipts total	321.79
Less: Payments total	(188.43)
Balance at the end of the week	693.97

When totalling the cash book columns always check your additions carefully as it is easy to make mistakes when totalling columns of numbers on a calculator. Check that the totals of each analysis column (excluding the discounts columns) add back to the total of the total column.

2 Preparing the bank reconciliation statement

2.1   Introduction

At regular intervals (normally at least once a month) the cashier must check that the cash book is correct by comparing the cash book with the bank statement.

2.2   Differences between the cash book and bank statement

At any date the balance shown on the bank statement is unlikely to agree with the balance in the cash book for two main reasons.

(a) **Items in the cash book not on the bank statement**

Certain items will have been entered in the cash book but will not appear on the bank statement at the time of the reconciliation. Examples are:

- Cheques received by the business and paid into the bank which have not yet appeared on the bank statement, due to the time lag of the clearing system. These are known as **outstanding lodgements** (can also be referred to as "uncleared lodgements").

- Cheques written by the business but which have not yet appeared on the bank statement, because the recipients have not yet paid them in, or the cheques are in the clearing system. These are known as **unpresented cheques**.

- Errors in the cash book (e.g. transposition of numbers, addition errors).

(b) **Items on the bank statement not in the cash book**

At the time of the bank reconciliation certain items will appear on the bank statement that have not yet been entered into the cash book. These can occur due to the cashier not being aware of the existence of these items until receiving the bank statements. Examples are:

- Direct debit or standing order payments that are in the bank statement but have not yet been entered in the cash payments book.

- BACS or other receipts paid directly into the bank account by a customer.

- Bank charges or bank interest that are unknown until the bank statement has been received and therefore will not be in the cash book.

- Errors in the cash book that may only come to light when the cash book entries are compared to the bank statement.

- Returned cheques i.e. cheques paid in from a customer who does not have sufficient funds in his bank to pay the cheque (see later in this chapter).

2.3 The bank reconciliation

🔍 Definition

Definition: A bank reconciliation is simply a statement that explains the differences between the balance in the cash book and the balance on the bank statement at a particular date.

A bank reconciliation is produced by following a standard set of steps.

Step 1: Compare the cash book and the bank statement for the relevant period and identify any differences between them.

You should begin with agreeing the opening balances on the bank statement and cash book so that you are aware of any prior period reconciling items that exist.

This is usually done by ticking in the cash book and bank statement items that appear in both the cash book and the bank statement. Any items left unticked therefore only appear in one place, either the cash book or the bank statement. We saw in 2.2 above the reasons why this might occur.

Step 2: Update the cash book for any items that appear on the bank statement that have not yet been entered into the cash book.

Tick these items in both the cash book and the bank statement once they are entered in the cash book.

At this stage there will be no unticked items on the bank statement.

(You clearly cannot enter on the bank statement items in the cash book that do not appear on the bank statement – the bank prepares the bank statement, not you. These items will either be unpresented cheques or outstanding lodgements – see 2.2 above.)

Step 3: Bring down the new cash book balance following the adjustments in step 2 above.

Step 4: Prepare the bank reconciliation statement.

This will typically have the following proforma.

Bank reconciliation as at 31.0X.200X

	£
Balance as per bank statement	X
Less unpresented cheques	(X)
Add outstanding lodgements	X
Balance as per cash book	X

Think for a moment to ensure you understand this proforma.

We deduct the unpresented cheques (cheques already entered in the cash book but not yet on the bank statement) from the bank balance, because when they are presented this bank balance will be reduced.

We add outstanding lodgements (cash received and already entered in the cash book) because when they appear on the bank statement they will increase the bank balance.

It is also useful to remember that the bank reconciliation can be performed the opposite way round as shown below:

Bank reconciliation as at 31.0X.200X

	£
Balance as per cash book	X
Add unpresented cheques	(X)
Less outstanding lodgements	X
	___
Balance as per bank statement	X
	___

If we start with the cash book balance, to reconcile this to the bank statement balance we add back the unpresented cheques as though they haven't been paid out of the cash book (as the bank statement has not recognised these being paid out).

We deduct outstanding lodgements as though we haven't recognised these in the cash book (as the bank statement has not recognised these receipts). The cash book balance should then agree to the bank statement balance i.e. we have reconciled these balances.

2.4 Debits and credits in bank statements

When comparing the cash book to the bank statement it is easy to get confused with debits and credits.

- When we pay money into the bank, we debit our cash book but the bank credits our account.

- This is because a debit in our cash book represents the increase in our asset 'cash'. For the bank, the situation is different: they will debit their cash book and credit our account because they now owe us more money; we are a payable.

- When our account is overdrawn, we owe the bank money and consequently our cash book will show a credit balance. For the bank an overdraft is a debit balance.

On the bank statement a credit is an amount of money paid into the account and a debit represents a payment. A bank statement conveys the transactions in the bank's point of view rather than the business' point of view.

Example

Given below are the completed cash books for Jupiter Limited from the previous example.

Cash receipts book

Date	Narrative		Total £	Sales tax £	SLCA £	Other £	Discount £
20X1							
2 July	Hill and French	40012	45.90		45.90		
3 July	Cash	40013	30.00			30.00	
4 July	Green and Holland	40014	245.89		245.89		3.68
			321.79	–	291.79	30.00	3.68

Cash payments book

Date	Details	Cheque	Code no	Total £	Sales tax £	PLCA £	Cash purchases £	Other £	Discounts received £
20X1									
2 July	Salary error	100107		56.89				56.89	
3 July	Preston Bros	100108		96.65		96.65			1.65
5 July	Petty cash	100109		34.89				34.89	
				188.43	–	96.65	–	91.78	1.65

You have now received the bank statement for the week commencing 1 July 20X1 which is also shown below.

FIRST NATIONAL BANK
Cheque Account
SHEET NUMBER 012
ACCOUNT NUMBER 38 41 57 33794363

			Paid in £	Paid out £	Balance £
28 June	Balance brought forward				560.61
1 July	CT	A/C 38562959	123.90		684.51
4 July	CHQ	100107		56.89	
4 July	CR	40013	30.00		657.62
5 July	CR	40012	45.90		
5 July	DR	Bank charges		5.23	
5 July	DD	English Telecom		94.00	
5 July	CHQ	100109		34.89	569.40

CHQ	Cheque	CT	Credit transfer	CR	Payment in
DR	Payment out	DD	Direct debit		

You are required to compare the cash book and the bank statement and determine any differences. Tick the items in the bank statement and in the cash book above, then prepare the bank reconciliation statement at 5 July 20X1.

The balance on the cash book at 28 June was £560.61.

Solution

Step 1   The cash book, duly ticked, appears below.

Cash receipts book

Date	Narrative		Total £	Sales tax £	SLCA £	Other £	Discount £
20X1							
2 July	Hill and French	40012	45.90 ✓		45.90		
3 July	Cash	40013	30.00 ✓			30.00	
4 July	Green and Holland	40014	245.89		245.89		3.68
			────	────	────	────	────
			321.79	–	291.79	30.00	3.68
			────	────	────	────	────

Cash payments book

Date	Details	Cheque	Code no	Total £	Sales tax £	PLCA £	Cash purchases £	Other £	Discounts received £
20X1									
2 July	Salary error	100107		56.89 ✓				56.89	
3 July	Preston Bros	100108		96.65		96.65			1.65
5 July	Petty cash	100109		34.89 ✓				34.89	
				188.43	–	96.65	–	91.78	1.65

The bank statement should have been ticked as shown below.

FIRST NATIONAL BANK
Cheque Account
SHEET NUMBER 012
ACCOUNT NUMBER 38 41 57 33794363

			Paid in £	Paid out £	Balance £
28 June	Balance brought forward				560.61
1 July	CT	A/C 38562959	123.90		684.51
4 July	CHQ	100107		56.89 ✓	
4 July	CR	40013	30.00 ✓		657.62
5 July	CR	40012	45.90 ✓		
5 July	DR	Bank charges		5.23	
5 July	DD	English Telecom		94.00	
5 July	CHQ	100109		34.89 ✓	569.40

CHQ	Cheque	CT	Credit transfer	CR	Payment in
DR	Payment out	DD	Direct debit		

Step 2 A comparison of the items in the cash book with those in the bank statement reveals unticked items in both.

(a) We will first consider the items that are unticked on the bank statement;

- there is a credit transfer on 1 July of £123.90 – this must be checked to the related documentation and then entered into the cash receipts book;

- the bank charges of £5.23 must be entered into the cash payments book;

- the direct debit of £94.00 should be checked and then entered into the cash payments book.

(b) We will now consider the items that are unticked in the cash book. Remember that no adjustment is needed to these but we have to decide where they will appear in the bank reconciliation statement.

- the cheque paid in on 4 July has not yet appeared on the bank statement due to the time it takes for cheques to clear through the clearing system – an outstanding lodgement;

- cheque number 100108 has not yet cleared through the banking system – an unpresented cheque.

The cash receipts and cash payments book will now appear as follows after the adjustments in (a) above.

Cash receipts book

Date	Narrative		Total	Sales tax	SLCA	Other	Discount
			£	£	£	£	£
20X1							
2 July	Hill and French	40012	45.90 ✓		45.90		
3 July	Cash	40013	30.00 ✓			30.00	
4 July	Green and Holland	40014	245.89		245.89		3.68
1 July	Credit transfer		123.90 ✓		123.90		
			445.69	–	415.69	30.00	3.68

Cash payments book

Date	Details	Cheque	Code no	Total	Sales tax	PLCA	Cash purchases	Other	Discounts received
				£	£	£	£	£	£
20X1									
2 July	Salary error	100107		56.89 ✓				56.89	
3 July	Preston Bros	100108		96.65		96.65			1.65
5 July	Petty cash	100109		34.89 ✓				34.89	
5 July	Bank charges			5.23 ✓				5.23	
5 July	English Telecom	DD		94.00 ✓		94.00			
				287.66	–	190.65	–	97.01	1.65

Note that the items we have entered in the cash book from the bank statement are ticked in both. There are no unticked items on the bank statement (not shown) and two unticked items in the cash book.

Step 3 Find the amended cash book balance.

	£
Balance at 28 June	560.61
Cash receipts in first week of July	445.69
Cash payments in first week of July	(287.66)
Balance at 5 July	718.64

Step 4 Reconcile the amended cash book balance to the bank statement balance.

Bank reconciliation as at 5 July 20X1

	£
Balance per bank statement	569.40
Less: unpresented cheque	(96.65)
Add: outstanding lodgement	245.89
Balance per cash book	718.64

This is the completed bank reconciliation.

Activity 2

The following are summaries of the cash receipts book, cash payments book and bank statement for the first two weeks of trading of Gambank, a firm specialising in selling cricket bats.

Cash receipts book

Date	Narrative	Total £	Sales tax £	SLCA £	Other £	Discount £
20X0						
01 Jan	Capital	2,000			2,000	
05 Jan	A Hunter	1,000		1,000		
09 Jan	Cancel cheque no 0009	90				90
10 Jan	I M Dunn	4,800		4,800		

Cash payments book

Date	Details	Cheque no	Code	Total £	Sales tax £	PLCA £	Cash purchases £	Other £	Discounts received £
20X0									
01 Jan	Wages	0001		50				50	
01 Jan	Fine	0002		12				12	
03 Jan	Dodgy Dealers	0003		1,500		1,500			
04 Jan	E L Pubo	0004		45		45			
05 Jan	Drawings	0005		200				200	
07 Jan	E L Wino	0007		30		30			
08 Jan	Toby	0008		1,400		1,400			
09 Jan	El Pubo	0009		70		70			
10 Jan	Marion's Emp	0010		200		200			
11 Jan	Speeding Fine	0011		99				99	

FINANCIAL BANK plc   CONFIDENTIAL

YOU CAN BANK ON US

10 Yorkshire Street   Account CURRENT   Sheet no. 1
Headingley   GAMBANK
Leeds LS1 1QT
Telephone: 0113 633061

Statement date 14 Jan 20X0   Account Number 40023986

Date	Details		Withdrawals (£)	Deposits (£)	Balance (£)
01 Jan	CR			2,000	2,000
02 Jan	0001		50		1,950
04 Jan	0003		1,500		450
05 Jan	0005		200		250
07 Jan	CR			1,000	
	0002		12		
	0004		45		
	0006		70		1,123
08 Jan	0007		30		1,093
10 Jan	0009		70		
	0009			70	
	0010		200		893
11 Jan	0012		20		
	Charges		53		820

SO	Standing order	DD	Direct debit	CR	Credit
AC	Automated cash	OD	Overdrawn	TR	Transfer

Prepare a bank reconciliation statement at 14 January 20X0.

2.5   Opening balances disagree

Usually the balances on the bank statement and in the cash book do not agree at the start of the period for the same reasons that they do not agree at the end, e.g. items in the cash book that were not on the bank statement. When producing the reconciliation statement it is important to take this opening difference into account.

Example

The bank statement and cash book of Jones for the month of December 20X8 start as follows.

	Bank statement	Debit £	Credit £	Balance £
1 Dec 20X8	Balance b/d (favourable)			8,570
2 Dec 20X8	0073	125		
2 Dec 20X8	0074	130		
3 Dec 20X8	Sundries		105	

Cash book

	£		£
1 Dec 20X8 b/d	8,420	Cheque 0075 Wages	200
Sales	320	Cheque 0076 Rent	500
	X		X
	X		X

Required:

Explain the difference between the opening balances.

Solution

The difference in the opening balance is as follows.

£8,570 – £8,420 = £150

This difference is due to the following.

	£
Cheque 0073	125
Cheque 0074	130
	255
Lodgement (sundries)	(105)
	150

These cheques and lodgements were in the cash book in November, but only appear on the bank statement in December. They will therefore be matched and ticked against the entries in the November cash book. The December reconciliation will then proceed as normal.

 Returned cheques

A customer C may send a cheque in payment of an invoice without having sufficient funds in his account with Bank A.

The seller S who receives the cheque will pay it into his account with Bank B and it will go into the clearing system. Bank B will credit S's account with the funds in anticipation of the cheque being honoured.

Bank A however will not pay funds into the S's account with Bank B and Bank B will then remove the funds from S's account.

The net effect of this is that on S's bank statement, the cheque will appear as having been paid in (a credit on the bank statement), and then later will appear as having been paid out (a debit on the bank statement).

The original credit on the bank statement will be in S's cash book as a debit in the normal way. But the debit on the bank statement (the dishonour of the cheque) will not be in S's cash book. This will have to be credited into the cash book as money paid out.

These cheques are technically referred to as 'returned cheques', but they are also called 'dishonoured cheques' or 'bounced cheques'.

Example

C sends a cheque to S in payment of an invoice for £300.

(a)   S will enter this cheque into his accounts as follows: Cash book

Cash book

	£		£
SLCA	300		

SLCA

	£		£
		Cash book	300

The cheque will appear on S's bank statement as a credit entry.

(b)   When the cheque is dishonoured S will enter this cheque into his accounts as follows:

Cash book

	£		£
		SLCA	300

SLCA

	£		£
Cash book	300		

The journal entry will be

Dr   SLCA   300

Cr   Cash book   300

This reinstates the receivable.

The dishonoured cheque will appear on the bank statement as a debit entry.

4   Summary

In this chapter you have had to write up the cash receipts and cash payments books and then total and balance the cash book. However, most importantly for this unit a comparison has to be made between the cash book and the bank statement and a bank reconciliation prepared. Do note that when comparing the bank statement to the cash book, figures appearing on the bank statement may be from the cash book some time ago due to the nature of the clearing system.

Answers to chapter activities

Activity 1

	£
Opening balance	(673.42)
Payments	(6,419.37)
Receipts	6,488.20
Closing balance	(604.59)

The closing balance is £604.59 overdrawn.

Activity 2

Step 1   Tick the cash books and bank statement to indicate the matched items.

Cash receipts book

Date	Narrative	Total	Sales tax	Sales ledger	Other	Discount
		£	£	£	£	£
20X0						
01 Jan	Capital	2,000 ✓			2,000	
05 Jan	A Hunter	1,000 ✓		1,000		
09 Jan	Cancel cheque no 0009	90				90
10 Jan	I M Dunn	4,800		4,800		
		7,890	–	5,800	2,090	–

Cash payments book

Date	Details	Cheque no	Code	Total £	Sales tax £	Purchases ledger £	Cash purchases £	Other £	Discounts received £
20X0									
01 Jan	Wages	0001		50	✓			50	
01 Jan	Fine	0002		12	✓			12	
03 Jan	Dodgy Dealers	0003		1,500	✓	1,500			
04 Jan	E L Pubo	0004		45	✓	45			
05 Jan	Drawings	0005		200	✓			200	
07 Jan	E L Wino	0007		30	✓	30			
08 Jan	Toby	0008		1,400		1,400			
09 Jan	El Pubo	0009		70	✓	70			
10 Jan	Marion's Emp	0010		200	✓	200			
11 Jan	Speeding Fine	0011		99				99	
				3,606	–	3,245	–	361	

FINANCIAL BANK plc				CONFIDENTIAL	

fb

YOU CAN BANK ON US

10 Yorkshire Street
Headingley
Leeds LS1 1QT
Telephone: 0113 633061

Account   CURRENT
       GAMBANK

Sheet no.   1

Statement date 14 Jan 20X0   *Account Number* 40023986

Date	Details		Withdrawals (£)	Deposits (£)	Balance (£)
01 Jan	CR			2,000✓	2,000
02 Jan	0001		50✓		1,950
04 Jan	0003		1,500✓		450
05 Jan	0005		200✓		250
07 Jan	CR			1,000✓	
	0002		12✓		
	0004		45✓		
	0006		70		1,123
08 Jan	0007		30✓		1,093
10 Jan	0009		70✓		
	0009			70	
	0010		200✓		893
11 Jan	0012		20		
	Charges		53		820

SO	Standing order	DD	Direct debit	CR	Credit
AC	Automated cash	OD	Overdrawn	TR	Transfer

Step 2   Deal with each of the unticked items.

Cash receipts book   –   cheque number 0009 does appear to have been cancelled as it has appeared as a debit and a credit entry in the bank statement – however the bank statement shows that the cheque was for £70 and not the £90 entered into the cash receipts book – this must be amended in the cash book.

–   the receipt from I M Dunn has not yet cleared through the banking system and is therefore not on the bank statement – it is an outstanding lodgement.

Cash payments book – cheque number 0008 to Toby and cheque number 0011 have not yet cleared through the clearing system – they are unpresented cheques.

Bank statement – cheque number 0006 has not been entered into the cash payments book but it has cleared the bank account – the cash book must be amended to show this payment.

– cheque number 0012 has not been entered into the cash payments book but it has cleared the bank account – the cash book must be amended to show this payment.

– the bank charges of £53 must be entered into the cash payments book.

Step 3 Amend the cash books and total them. Cash receipts book

Cash receipts book

Date	Narrative	Total £	Sales tax £	Sales ledger £	Other £	Discount £
20X0						
01 Jan	Capital	2,000 ✓			2,000	
05 Jan	A Hunter	1,000 ✓		1,000		
09 Jan	Cancel cheque no 0009	90			90	
10 Jan	I M Dunn	4,800		4,800		
10 Jan	Cancelled cheque adjustment 0009	(20) ✓			(20)	
		7,870	–	5,800	2,070	–

Cash payments book

Date	Details	Cheque no	Code	Total £	Sales tax £	Purchases ledger £	Cash purchases £	Other £	Discounts received £
20X0									
01 Jan	Wages	0001		50	✓			50	
01 Jan	Fine	0002		12	✓			12	
03 Jan	Dodgy Dealers	0003		1,500	✓	1,500			
04 Jan	E L Pubo	0004		45	✓	45			
05 Jan	Drawings	0005		200	✓			200	
07 Jan	E L Wino	0007		30	✓	30			
08 Jan	Toby	0008		1,400		1,400			
09 Jan	El Pubo	0009		70	✓	70			
10 Jan	Marion's Emp	0010		200	✓	200			
11 Jan	Speeding Fine	0011		99				99	
6 Jan		0006		70	✓	70			
10 Jan		0012		20	✓	20			
11 Jan	Bank charges			53	✓			53	
				3,749	–	3,335	–	414	

Step 4 Determine the amended cash book balance

	£
Opening balance	–
Cash receipts	7,870
Cash payments	(3,749)
Amended cash book balance	4,121

Step 5 Reconcile the amended cash book balance to the bank statement balance

	£	£
Balance per bank statement		820
Add: outstanding lodgement		4,800
Less: unpresented cheques 0008	1,400	
0011	99	
		(1,499)
Amended cash book balance		4,121

5 Test your knowledge

Workbook Activity 3

Given below are the cash receipts book, cash payments book and bank statement for a business for the week ending 11 March 20X1.

Required:

- Compare the bank statement to the cash book.

- Correct the cash receipts and payments books for any items which are unmatched on the bank statement.

- Total the cash receipts book and cash payments book and determine the final cash balance

- Using the reconciliation proforma reconcile the closing balance on the bank statement to the closing cash balance

Cash receipts book

Date	Narrative	Bank	Sales tax	Receiv- ables	Other	Discount
20X1		£	£	£	£	£
7/3	Balance b/f	860.40				
7/3	Paying in slip 0062	1,117.85	84.05	583.52	450.28	23.60
8/3	Paying in slip 0063	1,056.40	68.84	643.34	344.22	30.01
9/3	Paying in slip 0064	1,297.81	81.37	809.59	406.85	34.20
10/3	Paying in slip 0065	994.92	57.02	652.76	285.14	18.03
11/3	Paying in slip 0066	1,135.34	59.24	779.88	296.22	23.12

Cash payments book

Date	Details	Cheque no	Code	Bank £	Sales tax £	Payables £	Cash purchases £	Other £	Discounts received £
20X1									
7/3	P Barn	012379	PL06	383.21		383.21			
	Purchases	012380	ML	274.04	45.67		228.37		
	R Trevor	012381	PL12	496.80		496.80			6.30
8/3	F Nunn	012382	PL07	218.32		218.32			
	F Taylor	012383	PL09	467.28		467.28			9.34
	C Cook	012384	PL10	301.40		301.40			
9/3	L White	012385	PL17	222.61		222.61			
	Purchases	012386	ML	275.13	45.85		229.28		
	T Finn	012387	PL02	148.60		148.60			
10/3	S Penn	012388	PL16	489.23		489.23			7.41
11/3	P Price	012389	PL20	299.99		299.99			
	Purchases	012390	ML	270.12	45.02		225.10		

FINANCIAL BANK plc   fb   CONFIDENTIAL

YOU CAN BANK ON US

10 Yorkshire Street   Account CURRENT   Sheet no. 00614
Headingley
Leeds LS1 1QT   Account name T R FABER LTD
Telephone: 0113 633061

Statement date 11 March 20X1   Account Number 27943316

Date	Details	Withdrawals (£)	Deposits (£)	Balance (£)
7/3	Balance from sheet 00613			860.40
	Bank giro credit L Fernley		406.90	1,267.30
9/3	Cheque 012380	274.04		
	Cheque 012381	496.80		
	Credit 0062		1,117.85	1,614.31
10/3	Cheque 012383	467.28		
	Cheque 012384	301.40		
	Credit 0063		1,056.40	
	SO – Loan Finance	200.00		1,702.03
11/3	Cheque 012379	383.21		
	Cheque 012386	275.13		
	Cheque 012387	148.60		
	Credit 0064		1,297.81	
	Bank interest		6.83	2,199.73

DD	Standing order	DD	Direct debit	CP	Card purchase
AC	Automated cash	OD	Overdrawn	TR	Transfer

BANK RECONCILIATION STATEMENT AS AT 11 MARCH 20X1

£

Balance per bank statement
Outstanding lodgements:

Unpresented cheques:

Balance per cash book   £

✎ Workbook Activity 4

Given below is the cash book of a business and the bank statement for the week ending 20 April 20X1.

Required:

Compare the cash book to the bank statement and note any differences that you find.

Cash Book

Date	Details	£	Date	Details	£
16/4	Donald & Co	225.47	16/4	Balance b/d	310.45
17/4	Harper Ltd	305.68	17/4	Cheque 03621	204.56
	Fisler Partners	104.67	18/4	Cheque 03622	150.46
18/4	Denver Ltd	279.57	19/4	Cheque 03623	100.80
19/4	Gerald Bros	310.45		Cheque 03624	158.67
20/4	Johnson & Co	97.68	20/4	Cheque 03625	224.67
			20/4	Balance c/d	173.91
		1,323.52			1,323.52

EXPRESS BANK

CONFIDENTIAL

High Street
Fenbury
TL4 6JY
Telephone: 0169 422130

Account   CURRENT   Sheet no. 0213

Account name   P L DERBY LTD

Statement date 20 April 20X1   Account Number 40429107

Date	Details	Withdrawals (£)	Deposits (£)	Balance (£)
16/4	Balance from sheet 0212			310.45 OD
17/4	DD – District Council	183.60		494.05 OD
18/4	Credit		225.47	
19/4	Credit		104.67	
	Cheque 03621	240.56		
	Bank interest	3.64		408.11 OD
20/4	Credit		305.68	
	Credit		279.57	
	Cheque 03622	150.46		
	Cheque 03624	158.67		131.99 OD

DD	Standing order	DD	Direct debit	CP	Card purchase	
AC	Automated cash	OD	Overdrawn	TR	Transfer	

Workbook Activity 5

Graham

The cash account of Graham showed a debit balance of £204 on 31 March 20X3. A comparison with the bank statements revealed the following:

		£
1	Cheques drawn but not presented	3,168
2	Amounts paid into the bank but not credited	723
3	Entries in the bank statements not recorded in the cash account	
	(i) Standing orders	35
	(ii) Interest on bank deposit account	18
	(iii) Bank charges	14
4	Balance on the bank statement at 31 March	2,618

Tasks

(a) Show the appropriate adjustments required in the cash account of Graham bringing down the correct balance at 31 March 20X3.

(b) Prepare a bank reconciliation statement at that date.

Workbook Activity 6

The following are the cash book and bank statements of KT Ltd.

Receipts June 20X1

CASH BOOK – JUNE 20X1				
Date	Details	Total	Sales ledger control	Other
1 June	Balance b/d	7,100.45		
8 June	Cash and cheques	3,200.25	3,200.25	–
15 June	Cash and cheques	4,100.75	4,100.75	–
23 June	Cash and cheques	2,900.30	2,900.30	–
30 June	Cash and cheques	6,910.25	6,910.25	–
		£24,212.00	£17,111.55	

Payments June 20X1

Date	Payee	Cheque no	Total £	Purchase ledger control £	Operating overhead £	Admin overhead £	Other £
1 June	Hawsker Chemical	116	6,212.00	6,212.00			
7 June	Wales Supplies	117	3,100.00	3,100.00			
15 June	Wages and salaries	118	2,500.00		1,250.00	1,250.00	
16 June	Drawings	119	1,500.00				1,500.00
18 June	Blyth Chemical	120	5,150.00	5,150.00			
25 June	Whitby Cleaning Machines	121	538.00	538.00			
28 June	York Chemicals	122	212.00	212.00			
			19,212.00	15,212.00	1,250.00	1,250.00	1,500.00

Bank Statement

Crescent Bank plc
High Street
Sheffield
Account: Alison Robb t/a KT Ltd
Account no: 57246661

Statement no: 721

Page 1

Date	Details	Payments £	Receipts £	Balance £
20X1				
1 June	Balance b/fwd			8,456.45
1 June	113	115.00		8,341.45
1 June	114	591.00		7,750.45
1 June	115	650.00		7,100.45
4 June	116	6,212.00		888.45
8 June	CC		3,200.25	4,088.70
11 June	117	3,100.00		988.70
15 June	CC		4,100.75	5,089.45
15 June	118	2,500.00		2,589.45
16 June	119	1,500.00		1,089.45
23 June	120	5,150.00		4,060.55 O/D
23 June	CC		2,900.30	1,160.25 O/D

Key:	S/O	Standing Order	DD	Direct Debit
	CC	Cash and cheques	CHGS	Charges
	BACS	Bankers automated clearing	O/D	Overdrawn

Task

Examine the business cash book and the business bank statement shown in the data provided above. Prepare a bank reconciliation statement as at 30 June 20X1. Set out your reconciliation in the proforma below.

Proforma

BANK RECONCILIATION STATEMENT AS AT 30 JUNE 20X1

£

Balance per bank statement
Outstanding lodgements:

Unpresented cheques:

_____

Balance per cash book   £

_____

WORKBOOK ACTIVITIES
ANSWERS

Practice Activities Answers

1   Accounting for sales – summary

Workbook Activity 8

(a) Cash receipts book

Cash receipts book							
Narrative	SL Code	Discount £	Cash £	Bank £	Sales tax £	Cash sales £	SLCA £
G Heilbron	SL04			108.45			108.45
L Tessa	SL15	3.31		110.57			110.57
J Dent	SL17	6.32		210.98			210.98
F Trainer	SL21			97.60			97.60
A Winter	SL09	3.16		105.60			105.60
Cash sales			240.00		40.00	200.00	
		12.79	240.00	633.20	40.00	200.00	633.20

(b) General ledger accounts

Sales tax account

£		£
	28/4 CRB	40.00

Sales ledger control account

£		£
	28/4 CRB	633.20
	CRB – discount	12.79

Sales account

	£		£
		28/4 CRB	225.60
			200-00

Discount allowed account

	£		£
28/4 CRB	12.79		

(Note that the total of the 'Discount' column is not included in the cross-cast total of £873.20. The discounts allowed are entered into the cash receipts book on a memorandum basis; the total at the end of each period is posted to the sales ledger control account and to an expense account.)

(c) **Subsidiary ledger**

H Heilbron   SL04

	£		£
		28/4 CRB	108.45

L Tessa   SL15

	£		£
		28/4 CRB	110.57
		CRB – discount	3.31

J Dent   SL17

	£		£
		28/4 CRB	210.98
		CRB – discount	6.32

F Trainer   SL21

	£		£
		28/4 CRB	97.60

A Winter   SL09

	£		£
		28/4 CRB	105.60
		CRB – discount	3.16

Workbook Activity 9

Cash receipts book						
Narrative	Discount £	Cash £	Bank £	Sales tax £	Cash Sales £	SLCA £
Irlam Transport		468.00		78.00	390.00	
Paulson Haulage		216.00		36.00	180.00	
Mault Motors		348.00		58.00	290.00	
James John Ltd	24.39		579.08			579.08
Exilm & Co	19.80		456.74			456.74
	44.19	1,032.00	1,035.82	172.00	860.00	1,035.82

Workbook Activity 10

	True/False
Documents can be disposed of as soon as the year end accounts are prepared *Explanation – Businesses must keep copies of business and financial documents as they can be inspected by tax authorities and used as evidence in legal action*	FALSE
Documents cannot be inspected by anyone outside the business *Explanation – Documents can be inspected by tax authorities in a tax or sales tax inspection*	FALSE
Documents can be used as legal evidence in any legal actions	TRUE
Businesses must keep an aged receivable analysis as part of their financial documents *Explanation – Many businesses do keep an aged receivables analysis but it is not necessary to do so*	FALSE
Businesses do not need to keep copies of invoices *Explanation – Businesses do need to keep copies of invoices as they can be inspected by tax authorities*	FALSE
Businesses need to keep copies of their bank statements available for inspection	TRUE

2 Accounting for purchases – summary

Workbook Activity 6

CASH PAYMENTS BOOK

Date	Details	Code	Discount £	Cash £	Bank £	Sales tax £	PLCA £	Cash purchases £	Other £
12/3/X1	Homer Ltd	PL12	5.06		168.70		168.70		
	Forker & Co	PL07	5.38		179.45		179.45		
	Purchases			342.00		57.00		285.00	
	Print Ass.	PL08			190.45		190.45		
	ABG Ltd	PL02	6.62		220.67		220.67		
	Purchases			200.40		33.40		167.00	
	G Greg	PL19			67.89		67.89		
			17.06	542.40	827.16	90.40	827.16	452.00	–

- ## General ledger

Purchases ledger control account

		£			£
12/3	CPB	827.16	5/3	Balance b/d	4,136.24
12/3	CPB – discount	17.06			

Sales tax account

		£			£
12/3	CPB	90.40	5/3	Balance b/d	1,372.56

Purchases account

		£			£
5/3	Balance b/d	20465.88			
12/3	CPB	452.00			

Discounts received account

		£			£
			5/3	Balance b/d	784.56
			12/3	CPB	17.06

- **Purchases ledger**

ABG Ltd   PL02

		£			£
12/3	CPB 03652	220.67	5/3	Balance b/d	486.90
12/3	CPB – discount	6.62			

Forker & Co   PL07

		£			£
12/3	CPB 03649	179.45	5/3	Balance b/d	503.78
12/3	CPB – discount	5.38			

Print Associates   PL08

		£			£
12/3	CPB 03651	190.45	5/3	Balance b/d	229.56

Homer Ltd   PL12

		£			£
12/3	CPB 03648	168.70	5/3	Balance b/d	734.90
12/3	CPB – discount	5.06			

G Greg   PL19

		£			£
12/3	CPB 03654	67.89	5/3	Balance b/d	67.89

Workbook Activity 7

Cash payments book

Narrative	Discount £	Cash £	Bank £	Sales tax £	Cash Purchases £	PLCA £	Expenses £
JD & Co		96.00		16.00	80.00		
LJ Ltd		240.00		40.00	200.00		
MK Plc		60.00		10.00	50.00		
TB Ltd	2.52		68.89			68.89	
CF Ltd	3.16		156.72			156.72	
Electricity			90.00				90.00
Stationery			84.00	14.00			70.00
	5.68	396.00	399.61	80.00	291.28	225.61	163.39

Workbook Activity 8

Sales tax control

	£		£
Sales returns (SRDB)	6,000	Sales (SDB)	80,000
Purchases (PDB)	42,000	Cash sales (CRB)	168
Cash purchases (CPB)	240	Purchases returns (PRDB)	1,920
Balance c/d	33,848		
	82,088		82,088
		Balance b/d (owing to HMRC)	33,848

3 Ledger balances and control accounts

Workbook Activity 9

Account name	Amount £	Dr ✓	Cr ✓
Cash	2,350	✓	
Capital	20,360		✓
Motor Vehicles	6,500	✓	
Electricity	800	✓	
Office expenses	560	✓	
Loan from bank	15,000		✓
Cash at bank	6,400	✓	
Factory equipment	14,230	✓	
Rent	2,500	✓	
Insurance	1,000	✓	
Miscellaneous expenses	1,020	✓	

Workbook Activity 10

(a)

Purchases ledger control account

	£		£
Cash paid	47,028	Balance b/f	5,926
Purchases returns	202	Purchases (total from PDB)	47,713
Discounts received	867		
Sales ledger control account (contra)	75		
Balance c/d (bal fig)	5,467		
	53,639		53,639

(b)

Sales ledger control account

	£		£
Balance b/f	10,268	Bank account	69,872
Sales (total from SDB)	71,504	Irrecoverable debts account	96
		Sales returns account (total from SRDB)	358
		Discounts allowed (total from discount column in CB)	1,435
		Purchases ledger control account (contra)	75
		Balance c/d (bal fig)	9,936
	81,772		81,772

Workbook Activity 11

(a) **Sales ledger control account**

		£			£
30 Sep	Balance b/f	3,825	30 Sep Irrecoverable debts account (2)		400
			Purchases ledger control account (4)		70
			Discount allowed (5)		140
			Balance c/d		3,215
		3,825			3,825
1 Oct	Balance b/d	3,215			

(b) List of sales ledger balances

	£
Original total	3,362
Add: Debit balances previously omitted (1)	103
	3,465
Less: Item posted twice to Sparrow's account (3)	(250)
Amended total agreeing with balance on sales ledger control account	3,215

Workbook Activity 12

(a)

Account name	Amount £	Dr ✓	Cr ✓
Purchase ledger control account	1,000.00	✓	
Purchases	1,000.00		✓

(b)

Account name	Amount £	Dr ✓	Cr ✓
Purchase ledger control account	9.00	✓	
Discounts received	9.00		✓

(c)

Account name	Amount £	Dr ✓	Cr ✓
Purchase ledger control account	300.00	✓	
Sales ledger control account	300.00		✓

Workbook Activity 13

(a)

Details	Amount £	Dr ✓	Cr ✓
Balance of receivables at 1 July	60,580	✓	
Goods sold on credit	18,950	✓	
Payments received from credit customers	20,630		✓
Discounts allowed	850		✓
Irrecoverable debt written off	2,400		✓
Goods returned from credit customers	3,640		✓

(b)

	Amount £
Sales ledger control account balance as at 31 July	52,010
Total of sales ledger accounts as at 31 July	54,410
Difference	2,400

(c)

	✓
Goods returned may have been omitted from the sales ledger	
Irrecoverable debt written off may have been omitted from the sales ledger	✓
Goods returned may have been entered twice in the sales ledger	
Irrecoverable debt written off may have been entered twice in the sales ledger	

Workbook Activity 14

(a)

Details	Amount £	Dr ✓	Cr ✓
Balance of payables at 1 July	58,420		✓
Goods bought on credit	17,650		✓
Payments made to credit suppliers	19,520	✓	
Discounts received	852	✓	
Contra entry with sales ledger control	600	✓	
Goods returned to credit suppliers	570	✓	

(b)

	Amount £
Purchases ledger control account balance as at 31 July	54,528
Total of purchase ledger accounts as at 31 July	52,999
Difference	1,529

(c)

	✓
Payments made to suppliers may have been understated in the purchase ledger	
Goods returned to suppliers may have been overstated in the purchase ledger	✓
Goods bought on credit may have been overstated in the purchase ledger	
Contra entry may have been omitted from the purchase ledger	

4 Suspense accounts and errors

Workbook Activity 4

(a) Error disclosed by the trial balance – a single entry

(b) Error disclosed by the trial balance – a transposition error

(c) Error NOT disclosed by the trial balance – a compensating error

(d) Error NOT disclosed by the trial balance – an error of commission

(e) Error disclosed by the trial balance – two entries on one side

(f) Error disclosed by the trial balance – a casting error

(g) Error NOT disclosed by the trial balance – double entry is correct, it is only the subsidiary sales ledger that hasn't been updated

(h) Error disclosed by the trial balance – an extraction error

KAPLAN PUBLISHING

Workbook Activity 5

Account name	Amount £	Dr ✓	Cr ✓
Rent	200	✓	
Motor expenses	200		✓

Account name	Amount £	Dr ✓	Cr ✓
Bank	1,600		✓
Suspense	1,600	✓	

Account name	Amount £	Dr ✓	Cr ✓
Discounts received	1,800		✓
Suspense	1,800	✓	

Account name	Amount £	Dr ✓	Cr ✓
Miscellaneous expenses	500	✓	
Suspense	500		✓

Account name	Amount £	Dr ✓	Cr ✓
Sales tax	100	✓	
Suspense	100		✓

Re-drafted Trial Balance

	£	£
Receivables	33,440	
Bank	1,200	
Sales		401,300
Stock	24,300	
Wages	88,400	
Telephone	2,200	
Motor car	12,000	
Sales tax		5,200
Electricity	3,800	
Rent	16,400	
Purchases	241,180	
Purchases returns		1,600
Sales returns	4,200	
Office equipment	5,000	
Capital		49,160
Motor expenses	4,840	
Discounts allowed	4,010	
Discounts received		4,210
Payables		20,000
Drawings	40,000	
Miscellaneous expenses	500	
	481,470	481,470

5 Payroll procedures

Workbook Activity 3

	£
Gross pay	368.70
Less: PAYE	(46.45)
NIC	(23.96)
Net pay	298.29

Workbook Activity 4

Account name	Amount £	Dr ✓	Cr ✓
Wages expense	5475	✓	
Wages control	5475		✓

Account name	Amount £	Dr ✓	Cr ✓
HM Revenue and Customs	1388		✓
Wages control	1388	✓	

Account name	Amount £	Dr ✓	Cr ✓
Bank	4087		✓
Wages control	4087	✓	

Gross wages control account

		£			£
31 May	Net pay – Bank	4,087	31 May	Gross – wages expense	5,050
	PAYE – HMRC	635	31 May	Emp'ers NIC – wages exp	425
	Emp'ees NIC – HMRC	328			
	Empl'ers NIC – HMRC	425			
		5,475			5,475

KAPLAN PUBLISHING

Wages expense account

		£			£
30 Apr	Balance b/d	23,446			
31 May	Gross – wages control	5,050			
	Emp'ers NIC – control	425	31 May	Balance c/d	28,921
		28,921			28,921
31 May	Balance b/d	28,921			

HM Revenue and Customs account

		£			£
19 May	CPB	760	30 Apr	Balance b/d	760
			31 May	PAYE – wages control	635
				Emp'ees NIC – control	328
31 May	Balance c/d	1,388		Emp'ers NIC – control	425
		2,148			2,148
			31 May	Balance b/d	1,388

6 Petty cash systems

Workbook Activity 5

Petty cash book

Receipts			Payments								
Date	Narrative	Total	Date	Narrative	Voucher no	Total	Postage	Staff welfare	Station-ery	Travel expenses	Sales tax%
						£	£	£	£	£	£
5/1/X1	Bal b/d	150.00	12/1/X1	Postage	03526	13.68	13.68				
				Staff welfare	03527	25.00		25.00			
				Stationery	03528	15.12			12.60		2.52
				Taxi fare	03529	12.00				10.00	2.00
				Staff welfare	03530	6.40		6.40			
				Postage	03531	12.57	12.57				
				Rail fare	03532	6.80				6.80	
				Stationery	03533	9.60			8.00		1.60
				Taxi fare	03534	19.20				16.00	3.20
						120.37	26.25	31.40	20.60	32.80	9.32

CHEQUE REQUISITION FORM

CHEQUE DETAILS

Date	12/1/X1
Payee	Cash
Amount £	118.04
Reason	To restore petty cash
Invoice no. (attached/to follow)	–
Receipt (attached/to follow)	PETTY CASHIER
Required by (Print)	PETTY CASHIER
(Signature)	
Authorised by:	

General ledger accounts

Postage account

		£		£
5 Jan	Balance b/d	248.68		
12 Jan	PCB	26.25		

Staff welfare account

		£		£
5 Jan	Balance b/d	225.47		
12 Jan	PCB	31.40		

Stationery account

		£		£
5 Jan	Balance b/d	176.57		
12 Jan	PCB	19.40		

Travel expenses account

		£		£
5 Jan	Balance b/d	160.90		
12 Jan	PCB	33.01		

Sales tax account

		£			£
12 Jan	PCB	7.97	5 Jan	Balance b/d	2,385.78

Workbook Activity 6

Voucher total

	£
02634	13.73
02635	8.91
02636	10.57
02637	3.21
02638	11.30
02639	14.66
	62.38

Cash total

		£
£10 note	1	10.00
£5 note	2	10.00
£2 coin	3	6.00
£1 coin	7	7.00
50p coin	5	2.50
20p coin	4	0.80
10p coin	1	0.10
5p coin	2	0.10
2p coin	3	0.06
1p coin	6	0.06
		36.62

Reconciliation of cash and vouchers at 22 May 20X1

	£
Voucher total	62.38
Cash total	36.62
	99.00

The reconciliation shows that there is £1 missing. More cash has been paid out of the petty cash box than is supported by the petty cash vouchers. This could be due to a number of reasons:

- A petty cash claim was made out for, say, £11.30 but mistakenly the amount given to the employee was £12.30.

- An employee borrowed £1 from the petty cash box for business expenses and this has not been recorded on a petty cash voucher.

£1 has been stolen from the petty cash box.

7 The banking system

Workbook Activity 5

The following problems exist on the cheques received:

Cheque from K T Lopez – not signed;

Cheque from L Garry – post dated;

Cheque from L Barrett – made out to wrong name;

Cheque from P Ibbott – more than six months old;

Cheque from J Lovell – discrepancy between words and figures.

Workbook Activity 6

	✓
The customer's name	
The customer's address	✓
The customer's credit card number	
The customer's credit limit	✓
The customer's credit card company	
The available amount the customer has to spend	✓

KAPLAN PUBLISHING

Workbook Activity 7

	True/False
When a cheque is banked the funds are available immediately *Explanation – Cheques need to go through a clearing process with funds normally available after 3 days*	FALSE
A bank cheque has to be passed to the bank of the issuer before the money becomes available	TRUE
The clearing process is quicker for a building society than for a bank *Explanation – The clearing process is either the same length of time or longer for building societies than for banks*	FALSE
Cheques can only be processed by banks, not building societies *Explanation – Building societies also offer banking services and so can process cheques*	FALSE
Dishonoured cheques are returned to the drawer	TRUE
The drawer has the right to stop a cheque right up until the banker pays it	TRUE

8 Bank reconciliations

Workbook Activity 3

Cash receipts book

Date	Narrative	Bank	Sales tax	Receiva bles	Other	Discount
20X1		£	£	£	£	£
7/3	Balance b/f	860.40✓				
7/3	Paying in slip 0062	1,117.85✓	84.05	583.52	450.28	23.60
8/3	Paying in slip 0063	1,056.40✓	68.84	643.34	344.22	30.01
9/3	Paying in slip 0064	1,297.81✓	81.37	809.59	406.85	34.20
10/3	Paying in slip 0065	994.92	57.02	652.76	285.14	18.03
11/3	Paying in slip 0066	1,135.34	59.24	779.88	296.22	23.12
	BGC – L Fernley	406.90✓		406.90		
	Bank interest	6.83✓			6.83	
		6,876.45	350.52	3,875.99	1,789.54	128.96

Cash payments book

Date	Details	Cheque no	Code	Bank £	Sales tax £	Payables £	Cash purchases £	Other £	Discounts received £
20X1									
7/3	P Barn	012379	PL06	383.21✓		383.21			
	Purchases	012380	ML	274.04✓	45.67		228.37		
	R Trevor	012381	PL12	496.80✓		496.80			6.30
8/3	F Nunn	012382	PL07	218.32		218.32			
	F Taylor	012383	PL09	467.28✓		467.28			9.34
	C Cook	012384	PL10	301.40✓		301.40			
9/3	L White	012385	PL17	222.61		222.61			
	Purchases	012386	ML	275.13✓	45.85		229.28		
	T Finn	012387	PL02	148.60✓		148.60			
10/3	S Penn	012388	PL16	489.23		489.23			7.41
11/3	P Price	012389	PL20	299.99		299.99			
	Purchases	012390	ML	270.12	45.02		225.10		
	Loan finance	SO	ML	200.00✓				200.00	
				4,046.73	136.54	3,027.44	682.75	200.00	23.05

FINANCIAL BANK plc   fb   CONFIDENTIAL

YOU CAN BANK ON US

10 Yorkshire Street	Account CURRENT	Sheet no. 00614
Headingley		
Leeds LS1 1QT	Account name T R FABER LTD	
Telephone: 0113 633061		

Statement date 11 March 20X1   Account Number 27943316

Date	Details	Withdrawals (£)	Deposits (£)	Balance (£)
7/3	Balance from sheet 00613			860.40✓
	Bank giro credit L Fernley		406.90✓	1,267.30
9/3	Cheque 012380	274.04✓		
	Cheque 012381	496.80✓		
	Credit 0062		1,117.85✓	1,614.31
10/3	Cheque 012383	467.28✓		
	Cheque 012384	301.40✓		
	Credit 0063		1,056.40✓	
	SO – Loan Finance	200.00✓		1,702.03
11/3	Cheque 012379	383.21✓		
	Cheque 012386	275.13✓		
	Cheque 012387	148.60✓		
	Credit 0064		1,297.81✓	
	Bank interest		6.83✓	2,199.73

DD	Standing order	DD	Direct debit	CP	Card purchase
AC	Automated cash	OD	Overdrawn	TR	Transfer

BANK RECONCILIATION STATEMENT AS AT 11 MARCH 20X1

	£
Balance per bank statement	2,199.73
Add: Outstanding lodgements:	
Paying in slip 0065	994.92
Paying in slip 0066	1,135.34
Less: Unpresented cheques:	
Cheque 012382	(218.32)
Cheque 012385	(222.61)
Cheque 012388	(489.23)
Cheque 012389	(299.99)
Cheque 012390	(270.12)
Balance per cash book (Total of bank receipts – total of bank payments)	£2,829.72

Workbook Activity 4

Cash book

		£			£
16/4	Donald & Co	225.47✓	16/4	Balance b/d	310.45✓
17/4	Harper Ltd	305.68✓	17/4	Cheque 03621	204.56
	Fisler Partners	104.67✓	18/4	Cheque 03622	150.46✓
18/4	Denver Ltd	279.57✓	19/4	Cheque 03623	100.80
19/4	Gerald Bros	310.45		Cheque 03624	158.67✓
20/4	Johnson & Co	97.68	20/4	Cheque 03625	224.67
			20/4	Balance c/d	173.91
		1,323.52			1,323.52

There are three unticked items on the bank statement:

- direct debit £183.60 to the District Council;

- cheque number 03621 £240.56 – this has been entered into the cash book as £204.56;

- bank interest £3.64.

Cheques 03623 and 03625 are unticked items in the cash book but these are payments that have not yet cleared through the banking system.

EXPRESS BANK   CONFIDENTIAL

High Street   Account   CURRENT   Sheet no.   0213
Fenbury
TL4 6JY   Account name P L DERBY LTD
Telephone: 0169 422130

Statement date 20 April 20X1   Account Number 40429107

Date	Details	Withdrawals (£)	Deposits (£)	Balance (£)
16/4	Balance from sheet 0212			310.45 OD
17/4	DD – District Council	183.60		494.05 OD
18/4	Credit		225.47✓	
19/4	Credit		104.67✓	
	Cheque 03621	240.56		
	Bank interest	3.64		408.11 OD
20/4	Credit		305.68✓	
	Credit		279.57✓	
	Cheque 03622	150.46✓		
	Cheque 03624	158.67✓		131.99 OD

DD	Standing order	DD	Direct debit	CP	Card purchase
AC	Automated cash	OD	Overdrawn	TR	Transfer

Workbook Activity 5

Graham

(a)

Cash account

	£		£
Balance b/f	204	Sundry accounts	
Interest on deposit account	18	Standing orders	35
		Bank charges	14
		Balance c/d	173
	222		222
Balance b/d	173		

(b)

BANK RECONCILIATION STATEMENT AT 31 MARCH 20X3

	£
	£
Balance per bank statement	2,618
Add Uncleared lodgements	723
	3,341
Less Unpresented cheques	(3,168)
Balance per cash account	173

Workbook Activity 6

BANK RECONCILIATION STATEMENT AS AT 30 JUNE 20X1

	£	£
Balance per bank statement		(1,160.25) O/D
Outstanding lodgements: 30 June		6,910.25
		5,750.00
Unpresented cheques: 121	538.00	
122	212.00	
		(750.00)
Balance per cash book (7,100.45+ 17,111.55 – 19,212.00)		£5,000.00

MOCK ASSESSMENT

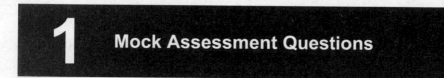

Mock Assessment Questions

SECTION 1

Task 1.1

Adams & Son's trial balance was extracted and did not balance. The credit column of the trial balance totalled £329,484 and the debit column totalled £327,231.

(a)   What entry would be made in the suspense account to balance the trial balance?

Account name	Amount £	Debit ✓	Credit ✓
Suspense			

It is important to understand the types of errors that are disclosed by the trial balance and those that are not.

(b)   Show which of the errors below are, or are not, disclosed by the trial balance.

Error in the general ledger	Error disclosed by the trial balance	Error NOT disclosed by the trial balance
Recording a bank payment for purchases on the debit side of both the bank and purchases account.	✓	✗
Recording a payment for rent and rates in a non-current assets account.		✓
Recording a sales invoice in the sales account only	✓	
Incorrectly calculating the balance brought down on the rent account.	✓	
Recording a receipt from a receivable in the bank account and the sales (subsidiary) ledger only	✓	
Recording payment of £1,300 in the bank account but £130 in the motor expenses account	✓	

Task 1.2

A credit customer, Foster's has ceased trading, owing Adams & Son £2,000 plus sales tax.

(a)   Record the journal entries needed in the general ledger to write off Foster's debt.

Select your account names from the following list: Adams & Son, Irrecoverable debts, Foster's, Purchases, Purchases ledger control, Sales, Sales ledger control, Sales tax.

Account name	Amount £	Debit ✓	Credit ✓

(b)   Adams & Son has opened up a new business Mini Adams. A new set of accounts are to be opened for Mini Adams, a partially completed journal to record the opening entries is shown below.

Record the journal entries needed in the accounts in the general ledger of Mini Adams to deal with the opening entries.

Account name	Amount £	Debit ✓	Credit ✓
Petty cash	100		
Bank (overdrawn)	5,000		
Capital	50,000		
Motor Vehicle	5,700		
Entertainment	340		
Bank loan	20,000		
Sundry expenses	320		
Computer equipment	7,653		
Stationery	201		
Heat & Light	3,478		
Journal to record the opening entries of new business – Mini Adams			

Task 1.3

Adams & Son pays employees by cheque every month and maintains a wages control account. A summary of last month's payroll transactions is shown below:

Item	£
Gross wages	18,708
Employers' NI	2,102
Employees' NI	1,782
Income tax	3,421
Trade Union fees	500

Record the journal entries needed in the general ledger to:

(a)   Record the wages expense.

(b)   Record the HM Revenue and Customs liability.

(c)   Record the net wages paid to the employees.

(d)   Record the Trade Union liability.

Select your account names from the following list: Bank, Employees NI, Employers NI, HM Revenue and Customs, Income tax, Net wages, Trade Union, Wages control, Wages expense.

(a)

Account name	Amount £	Debit ✔	Credit ✔

(b)

Account name	Amount £	Debit ✔	Credit ✔

(c)

Account name	Amount £	Debit ✔	Credit ✔

(d)

Account name	Amount £	Debit ✔	Credit ✔

Task 1.4

Adams & Son's initial trial balance includes a suspense account with a balance of £350.

The error has been traced to the sales returns day-book shown below.

Sales returns day-book

Date 20XX	Details	Credit note number	Total £	Sales tax £	Net £
31 July	Sloan's	231	2,400	400	2,000
31 July	Charlton & Bros	232	480	80	400
31 July	Matthew Manufacturers	233	1,200	200	1,000
	Totals		3,730	680	3,400

(a) Identify the error and record the journal entries needed in the general ledger to:

(i) Remove the incorrect entry.

(ii) Record the correct entry.

(iii) Remove the suspense account balance.

Select your account names from the following list: Charlton & Bros, Matthew Manufacturers, Purchases, Purchases day-book, Purchases ledger control, Purchases returns, Purchases returns day-book, Sales, Sales day-book, Sales ledger control, Sales returns, Sales returns day-book, Sloan's, Suspense, Sales tax.

(i)

Account name	Amount £	Debit ✓	Credit ✓

(ii)

Account name	Amount £	Debit ✓	Credit ✓

(iii)

Account name	Amount £	Debit ✓	Credit ✓

An entry to record a cash sale (ignore sales tax) of £190 has been reversed.

(b) Record the journal entries needed in the general ledger to:

(i) Remove the incorrect entry.

(ii) Record the correct entry.

Select your account names from the following list: Bank, Purchases, Purchases ledger control, Sales, Sales ledger control, Suspense, Sales tax.

(i)

Account name	Amount £	Debit ✓	Credit ✓

(ii)

Account name	Amount £	Debit ✓	Credit ✓

Task 1.5

When preparing the trial balance for Mini Adams, a suspense balance of £3,000 credit existed. All the bookkeeping errors have now been traced and the journal entries shown below have been recorded.

Journal entries

Account name	Debit £	Credit £
Heat and light	1,200	
Suspense		1,200
Suspense	4,200	
Rent and rates		4,200
Motor expenses	1,750	
Motor vehicles		1,750

(a) Post the journal entries to the general ledger accounts. Dates are not required.

Select your entries for the 'Details' column from the following list: Balance b/f, Heat and light, Motor expenses, Motor vehicles, Rent and rates, Suspense.

Heat and light

Details	Amount £	Details	Amount £

Rent and rates

Details	Amount £	Details	Amount £

Suspense

Details	Amount £	Details	Amount £
		Balance b/f	3,000

Motor expenses

Details	Amount £	Details	Amount £

Motor vehicles

Details	Amount £	Details	Amount £

Task 1.6

On 31 October, Adams & Son extracted an initial trial balance which did not balance, and a suspense account was opened. On 1 November journal entries were prepared to correct the errors that had been found, and clear the suspense account. The list of balances in the initial trial balance, and the journal entries to correct the errors, are shown below.

Re-draft the trial balance by placing the figures in the debit or credit column. You should take into account the journal entries which will clear the suspense account.

	Balances extracted on 31 October £	Balances at 1 November	
		Debit £	Credit £
Motor vehicles	47,284		
Fixtures and fittings	20,134		
Inventory	8,000		
Bank overdraft	1,231		
Petty cash	200		
Sales ledger control	105,872		
Purchases ledger control	67,980		
Sales tax owing to tax authorities	2,300		
Capital	50,000		
Sales	309,231		
Purchases	135,983		
Purchases returns	3,480		
Wages	60,131		
Motor expenses	2,312		
Office expenses	983		
Rent and rates	2,540		
Heat and light	3,214		
Insurance	2,100		
Miscellaneous expenses	1,781		
Suspense account (debit balance)	43,688		
Totals			

Journal entries

Account name	Debit £	Credit £
Sales	21,158	
Suspense		21,158
Sales	21,158	
Suspense		21,158

Account name	Debit £	Credit £
Rent and rates	686	
Suspense		686
Rent and rates	686	
Suspense		686

SECTION 2

Task 2.1

There are five payments to be entered in Adams & Son's cash-book.

Receipts

Received cash with thanks for goods bought.	Received cash with thanks for goods bought.	Received cash with thanks for goods bought.
From Adams & Son, a customer without a credit account.	From Adams & Son, a customer without a credit account.	From Adams & Son, a customer without a credit account.
Net £400	Net £320	Net £350
Sales tax £80	Sales tax £64	(No Sales tax)
Total £480	Total £384	
Johnson Ltd	*A Alpha*	*Bond's*

Cheque book counterfoils

ABC Ltd	Twilight
(Purchase ledger account ABC006)	(Purchase ledger account TWI001)
£2,000	
(Note: Have taken £20 settlement discount)	£240
000123	
	000124

(a)   Enter the details from the three receipts and two cheque book stubs into the credit side of the cash-book shown below and total each column.

Cash-book – credit side

Details	Discount	Cash	Bank	Sales tax	Payables	Cash purchases
Balance b/f						
Johnson Ltd						
A Alpha						
Bond's						
ABC Ltd						
Twilight						
Total						

There are two cheques from credit customers to be entered in Adam & Son's cash book:

Rhoda Ring   £560 (this customer has taken a £40 discount)

Reef   £210

(b)   Enter the above details into the debit side of the cash-book and total each column.

Cash book – debit side

Details	Discount	Cash	Bank	Receivables
Balance b/f		1,500	11,710	
Rhoda Ring				
Reef				
Total				

(c)   Using your answers to (a) and (b) above, calculate the cash balance.

£

(d)   Using your answers to (a) and (b) above, calculate the bank balance.

£

(e) Will the bank balance calculated in (d) above be a debit or credit balance?

Debit / Credit

Task 2.2

On 29 June Mini Adams received the following bank statement as at 24 June.

Assume today's date is 30 June, unless told otherwise.

Carlton Bank PLC

56 Armour Street, Rochdale, RO1 8YT

To: Mini Adams   Account No 82730193   24 June 20XX

Statement of Account

Date 20XX	Detail	Paid out £	Paid in £	Balance £	
06Jun	Balance b/f			12,000	C
06Jun	Cheque 11231	2,131		9,869	C
06Jun	Cheque 11232	123		9,746	C
07Jun	Cheque 11233	892		8,854	C
07Jun	Cheque 11234	2,141		6,713	C
07Jun	Bank Giro Credit Wright Bro's		1,532	8,245	C
12Jun	Cheque 11235	212		8,033	C
14Jun	Direct Debit Pink Panther	531		7,502	C
20Jun	Direct Debit Aldo Insurers	900		6,602	C
21Jun	Bank Charges	20		6,582	C
22Jun	Overdraft fee	15		6,567	C
24Jun	Paid in at Carlton Bank		300	6,867	C

D = Debit   C = Credit

The cash book as at 24 June is shown on the following page.

Cash book

Date 20XX	Details	Bank £	Date 20XX	Cheque number	Details	Bank £
01 June	Balance b/f	12,000	02 June	11231	Ally & Co	2,131
22 June	A Dude	300	02 June	11232	Mr Wong	123
23 June	XT Ltd	1,500	02 June	11233	Nina's Supplies	892
23 June	Maps Brothers	2,150	02 June	11234	Knobs & Bobs	2,141
			08 June	11235	PPP Ltd	212
			18 June	11236	Mama's Machines	2,350
			20 June	–	Aldo Insurers	900
			22 June	11237	George Richard's	5,000

(a) Check the items on the bank statement against the items in the cash book.

(b) Enter any items in the cash book as needed.

(c) Total the cash book and clearly show the balance carried down at 24 June (closing balance) and brought down at 25 June (opening balance).

Select your entries for the 'Details' column from the following list: A Dude, Aldo Insurers, Ally & Co, Balance b/d, Balance c/d, Bank charges, Closing balance, George Richard's, Knobs & Bobs, Mama's Machines, Maps Brothers, Mr Wong, Nina's Supplies, Opening balance, Overdraft fees, Pink Panther, PPP Ltd, Wright Bro's, XT Ltd

Note: You do not need to adjust the accounts in Section 1.

(d) Complete the bank reconciliation statement as at 24 June.

Select your entries for the 'Name' rows from the following list A Dude, Aldo Insurers, Ally & Co, Bank charges, George Richard's, Knobs & Bobs, Mama's Machines, Maps Brothers, Mr Wong, Nina's Supplies, Overdraft fees, Pink Panther, PPP Ltd, Wright Bro's, XT Ltd

Note: Do not make any entries in the shaded boxes.

Bank reconciliation statement as at 24 June 20XX

Balance per bank statement	£
Add:	
Name:	£
Name:	£
Total to add	£
Less:	
Name:	£
Name:	£
Total to subtract	£
Balance as per cash book	£

Task 2.3

This is a summary of petty cash payments made by Adams & Son.

Mary's Milk paid	£20.00 (no sales tax)
Cathy's Cabs paid	£24.00 (including sales tax)
Stu's Stationers paid	£40 plus sales tax

(a) Enter the above transactions, in the order in which they are shown, in the petty cash-book below.

(b) Total the petty cash-book and show the balance carried down.

Select your entries for the 'Details' columns from the following list: Amount, Balance b/d, Balance c/d, Cathy's Cabs, Details, Mary's Milk Post Office, Stationery, Stu's Stationers, Tea and coffee, Travel, Sales tax.

Petty cash-book

Debit side		Credit side					
Details	Amount £	Details	Amount £	Sales tax £	Tea and coffee £	Travel £	Stationery £
Balance b/f	100.00						

Task 2.4

Two amounts have been paid from petty cash:

- Paper for £12.00 including sales tax
- Motor expenses for £40.00 plus sales tax

(a) Complete the petty cash vouchers below.

Petty cash voucher	Petty cash voucher
Date: 8.07.XX Number: PC190	Date: 9.07.XX Number: PC191
Large pack of paper Net £ Sales tax £ Gross £	Fuel for AD's car Net £ Sales tax £ Gross £

Part way through the month, the petty cash account had a balance of £150.00 The cash in the petty cash box was checked and the following notes and coins were present.

Notes and coins	£
5 x £20 notes	100.00
5 x £5 notes	25.00
13 x £1 coins	13.00
10 x 50p coins	5.00
18 x 10p coins	1.80
15 x 5p coins	0.75

(b) Reconcile the cash amount in the petty cash box with the balance on the petty cash account.

Amount in petty cash box	£
Balance on petty cash account	£
Difference	£

At the end of the month, there were petty cash vouchers that totalled £167.34

(c) Complete the petty cash reimbursement document below to restore to an imprest amount of £200.

Petty cash reimbursement	
Date: 31.07.20XX	
Amount required to restore the cash in the petty cash box.	£

Task 2.5

This is a summary of transactions with customers of Mini Adams during the month of June.

(a) Show whether each entry will be a debit or credit in the sales ledger control account in the general ledger.

Details	Amount £	Debit ✔	Credit ✔
Balance of receivables at 1 June	69,876		
Sales made on credit	42,090		
Receipts from credit customers	32,453		
Discounts allowed	1,459		
Goods returned by credit customers	1,901		

(b)   What will be the balance brought down on 1 July on the above account?

	✓
Dr £ 69,876	
Cr £ 8,027	
Dr £ 76,153	
Cr £ 76,153	
Dr £ 111,534	
Cr £ 111,534	

The following debit balances were in the sales ledger on 1 July.

	£
Barr Ltd	23,453
Lou Lou	11,432
Grass Garden	1,200
Convent & Co	17,860
Trolls	18,080
Garvel	5,587

(c)   Reconcile the balances shown above with the sales ledger control account balance you have calculated in part (b).

	£
Sales ledger control account balance as at 1 July	
Total of sales ledger accounts as at 1 July	
Difference	

(d)   What may have caused the difference you calculated in part (c)?

✓

Goods returned may have been omitted from the sales ledger	
Discounts allowed may have been omitted from the sales ledger	
Goods returned may have been entered in the sales ledger twice	
Discounts allowed may have been entered in the sales ledger twice	

It is important to reconcile the sales ledger control account on a regular basis.

(e)   Which of the following statements is true?

✓

Reconciliation of the sales ledger control account assures managers that the amount showing as outstanding from customers is correct	
Reconciliation of the sales ledger control account assures managers that the amount showing as outstanding to suppliers is correct	
Reconciliation of the sales ledger control account will show if a purchase invoice has been omitted from the sales ledger	
Reconciliation of the sales ledger control account will show if a purchase invoice has been omitted from the purchases ledger	

Task 2.6

The following is an extract from Adam & Son's books of prime entry.

Totals for quarter

Sales day-book
Net: £156,000
Sales tax: £31,200
Gross: £187,200

Purchases day-book
Net: £80,000
Sales tax: £16,000
Gross: £96,000

Sales returns day-book
Net: £4,000
Sales tax: £800
Gross: £4,800

Purchases returns day-book
Net: £2,000
Sales tax: £400
Gross: £2,400

Cash book
Net cash sales: £1,000
Sales tax: £200
Gross cash sales: £1,200

(a)   What will be the entries in the sales tax control account to record the sales tax transactions in the quarter?

Select your entries for the 'Details' columns from the following list: Cash book, Cash Sales, Purchases, Purchases day-book, Purchases returns, Purchases returns day-book, Sales, Sales day-book, Sales returns, Sales returns day-book, Sales tax.

Sales tax control

Details	Amount £	Details	Amount £

The sales tax return has been completed and shows an amount owed to the tax authorities of £15,000.

(b)   Is the sales tax return correct?   Yes / No

Task 2.7

You will find that banks and building societies offer many similar services.

(a)   From the list below select TWO services that are offered by small mutual building societies and banks.

Service	Offered by BOTH banks & small mutual building societies ✔
An overdraft facility	
A savings account	
Foreign currency	
Safe custody	

(b)   Adams and Son received a cheque from a customer Polly Popper. Polly Popper banks with Le Banque Bank and Adams and Son banks with Carlton Bank PLC.

(i)   Who is the payee?

	✔
Adams and Son	
Polly Popper	
Carlton Bank PLC	
Le Banque Bank	

(ii)   Who is the drawer?

Adams and Son	
Polly Popper	
Carlton Bank PLC	
Le Banque Bank	

(iii)   Who is the drawee?

Adams and Son	
Polly Popper	
Carlton Bank PLC	
Le Banque Bank	

(c)   Match the description to the document

Aged receivable analysis	
Aged payable analysis	
Bank statements	
Remittance advice notes	

Provided to advise what invoices are being paid.
Provides a summary of all incomings and outgoings of the bank account.
Provides a breakdown of credit suppliers and amounts owed by the business by age.
Provides a breakdown of credit customers and amounts due to the business by age.

Task 2.8

Adams and Son receives payment from customers and makes payments to suppliers in a variety of ways.

(a)   From the list below, select what can be determined from the two different payment methods. (You can select more than one option, if necessary).

Checks to be made	Cheque	Credit card
Customer name		
Customer address		
Credit card number		
Cheque number		
The balance of the current account		
The remaining credit limit available		

(b) Show whether each of the statements below is true or false.

When Adams and Son makes payments to suppliers by credit card, the amount leaves the bank current account immediately.

    True / False

When Adams and Son makes payments to suppliers by debit card, the amount paid does not affect the bank current account.

    True / False

2 Mock Assessment Answers

SECTION 1

Task 1.1

(a)

Account name	Amount £	Debit ✓	Credit ✓
Suspense	2,253	✓	

(b)

Error in the general ledger	Error disclosed by the trial balance	Error NOT disclosed by the trial balance
Recording a bank payment for purchases on the debit side of both the bank and purchases account.	✓	
Recording a payment for rent and rates in a non-current assets account.		✓
Recording a sales invoice in the sales account only	✓	
Incorrectly calculating the balance brought down on the rent account.	✓	
Recording a receipt from a receivable in the bank account and the sales (subsidiary) ledger only	✓	
Recording payment of £1,300 in the bank account but £130 in the motor expenses account	✓	

Task 1.2

(a)

Account name	Amount £	Debit ✓	Credit ✓
Irrecoverable debts	2,000	✓	
Sales tax	400	✓	
Sales ledger control	2,400		✓

(b)

Account name	Amount £	Debit ✓	Credit ✓
Petty cash	100	✓	
Bank (overdrawn)	5,000		✓
Capital	50,000		✓
Motor Vehicle	5,700	✓	
Entertainment	340	✓	
Bank loan	20,000		✓
Sundry expenses	320	✓	
Computer equipment	7,653	✓	
Stationery	201	✓	
Heat & Light	3,478	✓	
Journal to record the opening entries of new business – Mini Adams			

Task 1.3

(a)

Account name	Amount £	Debit ✓	Credit ✓
Wages expense	20,810	✓	
Wages control	20,810		✓

(b)

Account name	Amount £	Debit ✔	Credit ✔
HM Revenue and Customs	7,305		✔
Wages control	7,305	✔	

(c)

Account name	Amount £	Debit ✔	Credit ✔
Bank	13,005		✔
Wages control	13,005	✔	

(d)

Account name	Amount £	Debit ✔	Credit ✔
Trade Union	500		✔
Wages control	500	✔	

Task 1.4

(a) (i)

Account name	Amount £	Debit ✔	Credit ✔
SLCA	3,730	✔	

(ii)

Account name	Amount £	Debit ✔	Credit ✔
SLCA	4,080		✔

(iii)

Account name	Amount £	Debit ✔	Credit ✔
Suspense	350	✔	

(b)   (i)

Account name	Amount £	Debit ✔	Credit ✔
Bank	190	✔	
Sales	190		✔

   (ii)

Account name	Amount £	Debit ✔	Credit ✔
Bank	190	✔	
Sales	190		✔

Task 1.5

(a)   Heat and light

Details	Amount £	Details	Amount £
Suspense	1,200		

Rent and rates

Details	Amount £	Details	Amount £
		Suspense	4,200

Suspense

Details	Amount £	Details	Amount £
Rent and rates	4,200	Balance b/f	3,000
		Heat and light	1,200

Motor expenses

Details	Amount £	Details	Amount £
Motor vehicles	1,750		

Motor vehicles

Details	Amount £	Details	Amount £
		Motor expenses	1,750

Task 1.6

	Balances extracted on 31 October £	Balances at 1 November Debit £	Credit £
Motor vehicles	47,284	47,284	
Fixtures and fittings	20,134	20,134	
Inventory	8,000	8,000	
Bank overdraft	1,231		1,231
Petty cash	200	200	
Sales ledger control	105,872	105,872	
Purchases ledger control	67,980		67,980
Sales tax owing to tax authorities	2,300		2,300
Capital	50,000		50,000
Sales (journal entry adjustment)	309,231		266,915
Purchases	135,983	135,983	
Purchases returns	3,480		3,480
Wages	60,131	60,131	
Motor expenses	2,312	2,312	
Office expenses	983	983	
Rent and rates (journal entry adjustment)	2,540	3,912	
Heat and light	3,214	3,214	
Insurance	2,100	2,100	
Miscellaneous expenses	1,781	1,781	
Suspense account (debit balance) (cleared)	43,688	–	–
Totals		391,906	391,906

SECTION 2

Task 2.1

(a) **Cash-book – credit side**

Details	Discount	Cash	Bank	Sales tax	Payables	Cash purchases
Balance b/f						
Johnson Ltd		480		80		400
A Alpha		384		64		320
Bond's		350		–		350
ABC Ltd	20		2,000		2,000	
Twilight			240		240	
Total	20	1,214	2,240	144	2,240	1,070

(b) **Cash book – debit side**

Details	Discount	Cash	Bank	Receivables
Balance b/f		1,500	11,710	
Rhoda Ring	40		560	560
Reef			210	210
Total	40	1,500	12,480	770

(c) £286

(d) £10,240

(e) Debit

Task 2.2

(a) to (c)

Date 20XX	Details	Bank £	Date 20XX	Cheque number	Details	Bank £
01 June	Balance b/f	12,000	02 June	11231	Ally & Co	2,131
22 June	A Dude	300	02 June	11232	Mr Wong	123
23 June	XT Ltd	1,500	02 June	11233	Nina's Supplies	892
23 June	Maps Brothers	2,150	02 June	11234	Knobs & Bobs	2,141
07 June	Wright Bro's	1,532	08 June	11235	PPP Ltd	212
			18 June	11236	Mama's Machines	2,350
			20 June	–	Aldo Insurers	900
			22 June	11237	George Richard's	5,000
			14 June		Pink Panther	531
			21 June		Bank charges	20
			22 June		Overdraft fee	15
			24 June		Balance c/d	3,167
		17,482				**17,482**
25 June	Balance b/d	3,167				

(d)

Balance per bank statement	£6,867
Add:	
Name: XT Ltd	£1,500
Name: Maps Brothers	£2,150
Total to add	£3,650
Less:	
Name: Mama's Machines	£2,350
Name: George Richard's	£5,000
Total to subtract	£7,350
Balance as per cash book	£3,167

Task 2.3

(a) and (b)

Petty cash-book

Debit side		Credit side					
Details	Amount £	Details	Amount £	Sales tax £	Tea and coffee £	Travel £	Stationery £
Balance b/f	100.00	Mary's Milk	20.00		20.00		
		Cathy's Cabs	24.00	4.00		20.00	
		Stu's Stationers	48.00	8.00			40.00
		Balance c/d	8.00				
	100.00		100.00	8.00	20.00	20.00	40.00

Task 2.4

(a)

Petty cash voucher	Petty cash voucher
Date: 8.07.XX Number: PC190	Date: 9.07.XX Number: PC191
Large pack of paper Net £ 10.00 Sales tax£ 2.00 Gross £ 12.00	Fuel for AD's car Net £ 40.00 Sales tax£ 8.00 Gross £ 48.00

(b)

Amount in petty cash box	£ 145.55
Balance on petty cash account	£ 150.00
Difference	£ 4.45

(c)

Petty cash reimbursement	
Date: 31.07.20XX	
Amount required to restore the cash in the petty cash box.	£167.34

Task 2.5

(a)

Details	Amount £	Debit ✔	Credit ✔
Balance of receivables at 1 June	69,876	✔	
Sales made on credit	42,090	✔	
Receipts from credit customers	32,453		✔
Discounts allowed	1,459		✔
Goods returned by credit customers	1,901		✔

(b)

	✓
Dr £ 69,876	
Cr £ 8,027	
Dr £ 76,153	✓
Cr £ 76,153	
Dr £ 111,534	
Cr £ 111,534	

(c)

	£
Sales ledger control account balance as at 1 July	76,153
Total of sales ledger accounts as at 1 July	77,612
Difference	1,459

(d)

	✓
Goods returned may have been omitted from the sales ledger	
Discounts allowed may have been omitted from the sales ledger	✓
Goods returned may have been entered in the sales ledger twice	
Discounts allowed may have been entered in the sales ledger twice	

(e)

	✓
Reconciliation of the sales ledger control account assures managers that the amount showing as outstanding from customers is correct	✓
Reconciliation of the sales ledger control account assures managers that the amount showing as outstanding to suppliers is correct	
Reconciliation of the sales ledger control account will show if a purchase invoice has been omitted from the sales ledger	
Reconciliation of the sales ledger control account will show if a purchase invoice has been omitted from the purchases ledger	

Task 2.6

(a) **Sales tax control**

Details	Amount £	Details	Amount £
Sales returns (SRDB)	800	Sales (SDB)	31,200
Purchases (PDB)	16,000	Cash sales (CB)	200
		Purchases returns (PRDB)	400
Balance c/d	15,000		
	31,800		31,800
		Balance b/d	15,000

(b)   Yes

KAPLAN PUBLISHING

Task 2.7

(a)

Service	Offered by BOTH banks & small mutual building societies ✓
An overdraft facility	
A savings account	✓
Foreign currency	✓
Safe custody	

(b)   (i)   Payee is Adams and Son

      (ii)   Drawer is Polly Popper

      (iii)   Drawee is Le Banque Bank

(c)

Aged receivable analysis	Provides a breakdown of credit customers and amounts due to the business by age
Aged payable analysis	Provides a breakdown of credit suppliers and amounts owed by the business by age.
Bank statements	Provides a summary of all incomings and outgoings of the bank account
Remittance advice notes	Provided to advise what invoices are being paid.

Task 2.8

(a)

Checks to be made	Cheque	Credit card
Customer name	✓	✓
Customer address		
Credit card number		✓
Cheque number	✓	
The balance of the current account		
The remaining credit limit available		

(b)   Show whether each of the statements below is true or false.

When Adams and Son makes payments to suppliers by credit card, the amount leaves the bank current account immediately.

False

When Adams and Son makes payments to suppliers by debit card, the amount paid does not affect the bank current account.

False

KAPLAN PUBLISHING

INDEX